The Great American Bologna Festival
and other student essays

A Celebration of Writing by Students Using
The St. Martin's Guide

Edited by

Elizabeth Rankin
University of North Dakota

St. Martin's Press
New York

For Information, Write:

St. Martin's Press, Inc.
175 Fifth Avenue
New York, NY 10010

ISBN: 0-312-05590-0

Acknowledgments

Scott Hyder, "*Poltergeist*, It Knows What Scares You," from *A Student's Guide to Freshman Writing*, 1989. Copyright 1989 by Burgess International Group Incorporated, Bellweather Press Division. Reprinted with permission.

Ilana Newman, "The Proposed English Language Amendment," from *A Student's Guide to Freshman Writing*, 1988. Copyright 1988 by Burgess International Group Incorporated, Bellweather Press Division. Reprinted with permission.

Connie Russell, "Let It Burn for the Next Generation," from *A Student's Guide to Freshman Writing*, 1989. Copyright 1989 by Burgess International Group Incorporated, Bellweather Press Division. Reprinted with permission.

Contents

Contents

Contents

Contents

Contents

vii

Contents

- **Chapter 1** -

Introduction

When I accepted the task of editing an anthology of student writing to accompany the third edition of the *St. Martin's Guide*, I didn't anticipate what a pleasure it would be. Imagine sitting down to read a set of papers and encountering there well over a hundred strong essays—essays that make a commitment to their subject, show evidence of sound research, impress you with their insights, and sometimes startle you with their eloquence.

Reading through them, I cannot help remembering my own college writing. Would it stand up to the best of these essays? Well, that piece on my childhood friend Cherry Ann wasn't bad. But the rest—well, the less said of that, the better.

The truth is, few writers—student or professional—write well on *every* subject. But once in a while there comes an occasion, an opportunity, that draws out the best in the writer. And on these occasions, our student writers often surprise us.

In this collection, you will find a number of surprises. Not all of the essays are perfect, of course. Many tease us with unfulfilled potential even in this "final" state. But all represent what students can do when they click with a writing assignment, when the chance to write coincides with the desire to say something significant.

Most of the essays in this volume were chosen from over 150 submitted by instructors or writing program directors at campuses across the country. A few of the essays were first pub-

1

lished in the Instructor's Resource Manual of the second edition of the *St. Martin's Guide*. In fact, it was because of the positive response to these essays, and to the student essays published in the *Guide* itself, that St. Martin's decided to assemble this collection of essays. All were written in response to assignments in the *Guide*.

In selecting the pieces for this collection, I have given consideration not only to overall quality, but to other factors as well. Because the essays are meant to serve as models to accompany the text, I was looking for pieces that would embody the basic features of each type of writing. And because the text is used by a variety of students in a variety of composition programs around the country, I also tried to choose essays that would reflect that variety—especially in regard to gender, geography, cultural background, and college type.

Despite these efforts to be objective, of course, I must admit that I have my own favorites here. I'm sure you'll find favorites too. And you may also find essays of your own that are at least as good, if not better, than those published here. When you do, we hope you'll submit them for possible inclusion in the next edition of this anthology. At the end of this collection, you'll find a paper submission form.

In the meantime, if you aren't already doing so, you might consider publishing your own anthology or holding a contest to celebrate the best student essays at your campus. Many schools do that already—and we have been fortunate to be able to include some of the award-winning essays from the Universities of Arizona, Cincinnati, Kentucky, and North Dakota. What better way to celebrate student writing than to make it available to a wider audience!

· Chapter 2 ·

Remembering Events

The essays in this section cover a wide range of experience, from a quiet departure for college in the Midwest, to a hunting episode in South Carolina, a forest fire in Montana, and, most dramatically, an escape from war-torn Afghanistan. Such disparate subjects obviously pose different challenges for the writer, and require different narrative techniques.

In the first essay, Scott Weckerly writes about a familiar subject for most college students — the experience of first leaving home. The challenge here is to avoid sentimentality, to draw out the subtlety and complexity in that experience. Weckerly manages this by creating an ironic distance from his youthful self, and by invoking in the final paragraph a powerful metaphor that allows the reader to feel his fear and excitement.

Tim Taylor chooses another fairly common subject — the initiation ritual that is so often embodied in a hunting story — but in this case the story takes an unexpected turn. Using the techniques of the dream sequence and the first-person present tense narrative so common in contemporary fiction, Taylor achieves a dramatic immediacy that leads the reader toward a moment of climax and then stops short, allowing the incident to open out, rich with unspoken significance.

Linda Lilly's narrative is more action than reflection, its drama heightened by the threat of death that the forest fire poses. Unlike Taylor, Lilly chooses a chronological sequence and past tense narrative, and her language, energized by strong verbs and powerful visual images, seems to carry us along at a much quicker pace.

Finally, we have Afghani immigrant Abida Wali's account of her family's dramatic escape from their homeland. For the most part, Wali chooses to underplay the drama, to let the events speak for themselves. Still, her artful choice of detail—as in a scene where she stumbles over the hem of a Chaderi—creates a vivid impression and helps us imagine ourselves in this exotic locale.

This last observation brings up an important point. One of the significant features of autobiographical writing is its ability to connect with the reader's experience. One might ask how Wali's essay does that. Perhaps we can answer this question by simply asking ourselves: Did I keep reading? Did I care what was happening? Having finished the essay, do I feel that my own experience is richer for it? If so, the writer *has* made that connection. As in so many things, it's less a matter of *what* is written about, than of *how* it is written.

Free Falling

. . .

Scott Weckerly

Southern Illinois University
Carbondale, Illinois

The impact of saying good-bye and actually leaving did not   1
hit me until the day of my departure. Its strength woke me an
hour before my alarm clock would, as for the last time Missy,
my golden retriever, greeted me with a big, sloppy lick. I hated
it when she did that, but that day I welcomed her with open
arms. I petted her with long, slow strokes, and her sad eyes
gazed into mine. Her coat felt more silky than usual. Of course,
I did not notice any of these qualities until that day, which
made me all the more sad about leaving her.

The entire day was like that: a powerful awakening of whom   2
and what I would truly miss. I became sentimental about saying good-bye to many people I had taken for granted—the
regulars who came into the restaurant where I worked, the
ones I never seemed to find time to speak with. I had to leave
all of my friends and also the classmates I had always intended
to "get to know someday." Most importantly, I would be forced
to say farewell to the ones who raised me.

All at once, the glorious hype about becoming indepen-   3
dent and free became my sole, scary reality. I began to feel the
pressure of all my big talk about being a big shot going to a big-
time school. Big deal. I had waited so impatiently for the day
to arrive, and now that it finally had, I felt as if I did not want

5

to go. I suppose that goes with the territory of enrolling in a university six hours from home.

Upon my decision to do so, in fact, all of my personal problems had seemed to fade. I didn't care; I was leaving. I wanted to make it clear to everyone that I *wanted* to go — and by God, I was ready. Then the day came, and I wondered if I was honestly ready to go. 4

My dad and stepmom were taking me to school, but first I had to say good-bye to my mom. No one ever said divorce was easy. I met Mom for brunch that morning, and she immediately began talking of my future experiences. More so, she talked a little of her first year away from home — cluttered dorm, shy roommate, some art history classes — and she spoke with such detail and enthusiasm that I clearly saw what a lasting impression college makes. We talked then of my expectations — what the guys on my floor would be like, how I hoped my classes would not be on opposite sides of campus, whether I'd gain weight on cafeteria food. 5

She paused for a second, and then quipped, "The food won't make you gain weight; the beer will." 6

I smiled. I felt relieved that Mom was in a cheerful mood, rather than a maudlin one. Ironically, the sky was filled with sunshine and bright, silky clouds. Somehow, I'd expected it to be gray and overcast. As we talked, I realized I would soon begin the long, complicated road to independence. The security I had selfishly taken for granted at home would eventually diminish into memory. Home would no longer be home, but Carbondale, Illinois. 7

When the waitress brought our bill, Mom's mood shifted noticeably. She became quiet, even somber. I suppose for her that somehow signalled the conclusion of our last meal together, at least the last one for quite some time. She looked down at the table pensively. Looking back now, I can see the significance that day probably had for my mother. As a parent, she must have been anticipating that day ever since November 30, 1971, and it surely challenged her emotionally. 8

She walked me to my car, and I could feel my sadness in the pit of my stomach. The summer breeze dried my eyes, and I blinked profusely to moisten them. 9

"Well, I guess I have to go," I mumbled, looking into the dis- 10
tance. I could not believe I did not have the courage to say that
directly into her eyes.

"I know," she replied with a faint smile and then quipped, 11
"It's not too late to change your mind." She was joking, but
there seemed to be some seriousness in her voice. Her smile
quickly faded when I said I couldn't.

"I'm going to miss you," she added. 12

"You make it sound as if you're never going to see me 13
again."

"You could call . . . collect, of course." 14

I laughed. The implication that all money spent from then 15
on would be my own was scary, yet funny as well.

"Don't worry about me too much, Mom." 16

"I'll miss you." She drew me close and gave me a hug, and I 17
assured her I'd be back sooner than she'd realize. She then told
me that she loved me.

"I . . . love you, too." The difficulty of saying those words 18
overwhelmed me. I had always seen myself as someone with
solid, untouchable emotions. At that moment, though, I was in
a fragile, quivering state; and I could not believe I had con-
jured such a false image of myself.

We drew apart, and I slowly climbed into my gray Maxima. 19
She did not cry, but who knows what happened when I turned
the corner. I don't think I want to know.

At that time, I felt like a rookie sky diver preparing for his 20
first plunge. The cabin door opens to reveal the extreme distance of his fall, which leads to either sheer excitement or
eventual death. The näiveté that sheltered his fear disappears
at the sudden reality of the moment. By then, of course, it is
much too late to turn back. The very thought that this was *his*
idea seems absurd to him, and he feels like the only person on
the face of the planet. And so he closes his eyes, takes a deep
breath, and jumps.

Confessions of a Deer Hunter

■　■　■

Tim Taylor

University of South Carolina
Columbia, South Carolina

Slowly the buck moves out of the thick cover of briers and short pine trees onto the old road bed. I raise my rifle and push the safety button to the fire position. Trying to hold the cross-hairs on the buck's massive shoulder, I begin to squeeze the trigger. Before I can fire, he bolts, startled by a loud buzzing noise—the sound of my alarm clock going off. 1

Half asleep, I fumble quickly to turn it off. It's 3:30 A.M. and there's no time to waste. I had prepared my hunting gear the night before: my camouflage pants, jacket, rainsuit, and insulated coveralls are on the couch in the den. After putting on my pants, I go to the back door to check on the weather, since the last few days have been unseasonably warm for November. Today is no exception. It's warm and cloudy so I take my rainsuit instead of the insulated coveralls. Then I call Byron to let him know I'm on my way. 2

When I get to his house, he's ready to go. I load my gear into his truck and we're off. Silently drinking the coffee and eating the ham biscuits I brought, I think about my dream and how easy the shot always seems in my dreams. But somehow I never fire. 3

It takes almost an hour to get to Dogwallow Road in Mableton. There we meet Byron's dad and Warren. Warren and I are 4

8

going to hunt the lower end of the property, close to the creek, while Byron and his dad go to the upper end near the oak trees. Using a flashlight, we make our way into the sleeping woods, crunching leaves loudly under our feet. I wonder how deer can move so silently. By 5:45, I settle comfortably into my deer stand, still an hour before daylight.

The stand is on the edge of an overgrown road that was 5 once used for logging. Leaning against a tree, the stand looks like a tall ladder with a chair on top. It's surrounded by tall pines, oaks, and poplars. From there I have a good view of three heavily used deer trails twenty-five yards up the road.

As dawn approaches, an owl hoots nearby. The woods 6 slowly come to life. Birds begin chirping and I think I hear squirrels growling at one another. A steady rain of leaves drifts down, covering the forest floor with patches of yellow, red, and orange. At the rate they're falling, I figure the forest will be bare in a few hours. I strain to hear the sound of a twig snapping or the shuffle of hooves in the leaves. Suddenly my attention is diverted by a woodpecker's tapping on a nearby tree. I look at him through my rifle scope. His bright red head is a blur as he moves rat-a-tat-tat against the tree. A sparrow lands in front of me. As we watch each other, he turns his head sideways quizzically, as if he's trying to figure out what I'm doing here. Satisfied or not, he hops and flies off.

After a while, I notice that the woods are strangely quiet. 7 The breeze has died down and the leaves are no longer falling. Relaxed, I begin to drift off to sleep. A movement near the deer trail wakens me with a start. Looking hard, I think I see legs through the thick brush. I raise my rifle and wait. Then I see them, a doe and two yearlings. I watch as they move. Every few minutes, the doe looks back. My hands tremble and my heart races. Then I hear it, moving through the woods at a tremendous speed.

Just like in my dream, the buck moves out of the bush and 8 onto the road. I see him clearly. He's magnificent. He turns and looks directly at me and I know it's the buck I've dreamed of since childhood. He's a twelve pointer, weighing over two hundred pounds. My heart is beating so loudly I know he's going to hear it. My arm shakes. I try to steady my aim. I catch my breath and start slowly to squeeze the trigger. Then I lower the gun. The buck flicks his tail and walks off into the cover of the woods.

I sit there wondering why I didn't shoot. When I've killed 9 deer before, I've had ambivalent feelings but they didn't stop me from shooting. Now I'm bewildered. Why didn't I shoot? What's different about this one?

Still trying to figure it out, I hear Warren come up behind 10 me. It's 10:00, he tells me, and Byron's dad needs to get back to go to work. I climb down out of my stand and we walk to the truck. Byron and his dad are already there. We talk about how noisy the leaves were and give reasons for not seeing any deer. I want to tell them about my buck, but they wouldn't understand why I didn't shoot. I don't understand myself.

At home that night, I make sure the alarm is set for 3:30 11 A.M. and drift off to sleep thinking about the peacefulness of the woods. It's a cold crisp morning with frost on the ground. The buck is standing on the knoll with his head held high. He's been running, and he's breathing hard. Looking at him now, I know why I didn't shoot and I'm glad.

One Blessed Acre

■   ■   ■

Linda Lilly

University of Idaho
Moscow, Idaho

The pea-green helicopter sailed through the morning air   1
over spans of roadless forest. It was a sweltering July morning,
and the breeze in the open-air chopper was exhilarating. I sat
sideways in the Army Huey with nothing but a seatbelt
between me and the sky.

We were in the Lewis and Clark National Forest near White   2
Sulphur Springs, a part of Montana that was new to me. From
the air, I could see rolling hills, spotted with large grassy
meadows here and there breaking up the thickly timbered
terrain. Facing north, the only evidence of the fire raging
behind us was the gray haze suspended around the peaks and
blanketing the valleys. The crew yawned and joked over the
copter's racket. John, our crew boss, strained to study the terrain, sizing up the day's assignment.

We veered to the south and circled back for a landing.   3
Dense smoke filled the sky. I could make out charred slopes
and occasional trees lit at the top like candles. An intense fire
front appeared to be moving our way. The fire had already
consumed five thousand acres.

We piled noisily out of the helicopter and greeted Larry,   4
our division boss. As one of three squad bosses, I was responsible for five Forest Service firefighters. I patted my pockets, web

belt, and butt pack to make sure I hadn't left any of my paraphernalia on the chopper.

Assessing the situation, John and Larry decided to take a   5
closer look at the fire heading in our direction. Not more than five minutes later, we heard John's voice on the radio: "Larry, this is too big and it's moving fast. Let's get out of here."

"Ten-four. I'll radio for release," Larry responded.   6

While waiting anxiously for them to return, we kept an eye   7
on the monstrous blaze that was approaching. When he got back, Larry breathlessly told us he had requested a chopper. As we waited, we could hear the sounds of bursting trees and popping needles becoming louder.

Finally the chopper pilot came over the radio: "Too much   8
smoke and wind to land. Better locate an escape route." For a moment, everyone was silent. I could hear my heart pounding in my chest.

Larry came back urgently, "What's ahead on this ridge? Is   9
there somewhere we can get to that's safe?"

"Well," the pilot responded, "I can't see clearly now, but I 10
remember seeing a clearing about a mile up the ridge. That's your best bet."

Without a moment to spare, John started barking orders: 11
"Get in line by squads and walk quickly up the ridge. Do not run! If you haven't read the instructions on your fire shelter, do it now."

That last order shook me. A fire shelter is an aluminum-   12
foil pup tent. You carry it around but hope never to use it. We call it the human hot-dog roaster. Somehow I had to keep calm, although the impulse to run was fierce. Walking beside the other members of my squad, I made sure that everyone knew what to do. The crew fell silent. All that could be heard was the distant roar of the fire and our own labored breathing as we trudged up the ridge.

A whoop from John let us know that we had found the   13
clearing. We converged on the top of a peak, a rocky acre with a few stunted pines and windswept junipers, but mostly boulders and broken shale. Relief was great, but not complete. The helicopter still couldn't get through but our rocky peak was virtually unburnable.

All we could do was sit and wait. I don't know which was   14
worse: scuttling up the ridge not knowing where we were going
or waiting on this peak with nowhere left to go. The less
experienced ones figured we were safe, that no one would
let anything happen to us now. They joked and ate. I munched
a sandwich, but it felt like ashes in my mouth. From the look
of things, the fire was going to go right over us. We'd have to
use our shelters and if the fire didn't get us, the smoke and
heat would.

My mind played with the thought that I might not see the   15
morning sun again. Thoughts of my husband and three children overwhelmed me. All I wanted was to hold them and have
them comfort me. I fought back tears. I inwardly raged against
the officials who had put us in this spot.

Larry and John realized morale was getting low and set us   16
to work clearing brush and cutting down trees—anything to
keep us from thinking about our predicament. People started
to snap out of their stupors. Some told strained jokes and we
made ourselves laugh.

After what seemed hours, the time arrived to deploy our   17
fire shelters. The sky turned a dark orange. Smoke blocked out
the sun, but we could see the wall of flames racing toward us.
It whipped up fire devils five hundred feet high and picked up
trees, flipping them in the air like toothpicks. The wind was so
strong that even though our hard hats were strapped under
our chins, they still hovered in the air above our heads. We
crouched behind the rocks trying to release the fire shelters,
our eyes half-closed from wind and smoke. The noise was
deafening. We could not speak to each other, but I could hear
our silent prayers rising to the heavens.

Then it passed. It was as if someone had reached out a   18
hand and cupped it around us. The fire passed not more than
two hundred feet away. Awestruck, we peered over the boulders
and witnessed nature at its most beautiful and ferocious—
uncontrollable energy churning, roaring, blowing at forty
miles an hour hundreds of feet into the air. Seconds later, it
met another fire storm coming from the opposite direction.
The meeting of the two was like an atomic bomb. Black billows
rolled outward and upward from a thick stem of smoke and

flame. The cloud rose so high that the fluffy top of the mushroom changed from black to white in the cooler upper atmosphere.

Suddenly, our silence broke. Yelling and laughing, we hugged each other as we watched the miraculous sight. Then, we heard the thap, thap, thap of helicopter blades slicing the thick air. That sandwich and Snickers would taste pretty good now, I thought as I climbed stiffly into my seat. As we whirred away, I looked down. The entire ridge we had hiked up only moments earlier was black and smoldering.

19

An Escape Journey

•   •   •

Abida Wali

University of California at San Diego
La Jolla, California

It was 11:30 P.M. in Kabul. We were all waiting for my uncle   1
to return from a meeting with his collaborators. Every night
before the curfew, they distributed *Shabnameh* (*The Night Letter*),
a pamphlet mimeographed or copied by hand and secretly left
in public places. Many people had been arrested, tortured,
imprisoned, and killed for the possession or distribution of
anti-regime *Night Letters*. Usually, my uncle got home by ten,
but now the clock was about to strike twelve midnight. What
could have happened? Had he been arrested? If he didn't get
home before the midnight curfew went into effect, he could
be shot.

Suddenly, a pounding at the door broke the silence. My   2
heart beat faster and faster as I rushed to the door. Who could
it be? Could it be my uncle — or soldiers coming to arrest my
dad after they arrested my uncle?

"Who is it?" I asked.   3

"Open the door," a voice replied from the other side of the   4
door. I didn't recognize the voice.

"Open the door," the voice repeated.   5

As I turned the knob, the person pushed the door open,   6
throwing me back against the wall. My uncle rushed into the
living room. I slammed the door and ran after him. Trembling

15

and gasping, he looked toward my dad and said "Abdulla and Ahmed have been arrested . . . they could have given my name under torture . . . I'm next."

"We have to leave immediately," my dad replied.　　　7

I helped my mom pack canned foods, clothing, and the　8 first aid kit. We were told to take only the things that we would need for our journey, but Mom slipped the family photo album between the clothes. After a frantic hour of rushing from room to room, gathering our supplies in bundles, we had to wait until the curfew was lifted at dawn. At the crack of dawn, we abandoned the house forever, setting out on an uncertain journey. As Mom shut the front door, she looked for the last time at her great-grandmother's tea pot.

We took a bus from Kabul to Nangarhar. Along the road to　9 Nangarhar were two or three checkpoints where soldiers would search the bus for arms and illegal documents. At the first checkpoint, a soldier got on the bus. From the hammer and sickle on his cap, I knew he was Russian. He wore a big army coat and held a rifle, an AK-47 Kalashnikov, to his chest. His boots shook and rattled the windows and the metal floor of the bus. Suddenly, he stopped, pointed his gun at a man, and signaled him to get off the bus. The man ignored him. The soldier stepped forward and tried to pull him out of the seat, but the man clung to the seat and wouldn't let go. My heart was racing. Drops of sweat were forming on my forehead. Finally, the man let go and was escorted by two other soldiers to a jeep parked beside the bus. The pounding of the boots against the bus floor started again, and this time, the soldier stopped at my dad and me.

"Where are you going?" he asked.　　　10

"To my uncle's funeral in Nangarhar," Dad answered.　11

"Your ID?"　　　12

Dad gave him his ID. The soldier opened it to see the pic-　13 ture. I felt a drop of sweat drop from my forehead. Finally, the soldier handed back the ID. He looked around the bus once more and gave the driver permission to pass.

We made the rest of the journey in fear of getting blown up　14 by anti-personnel mines. I saw six passenger buses that had been destroyed by mines on the road to Nangarhar. Finally, after eight hours of travelling, which should have been four, we reached Nangarhar.

From the bus station we took a taxi to a friend's house and 15 waited there two days for someone to smuggle us across the border. After two days my dad's friend introduced us to the Smuggler. His six-foot height, bushy beard, upturned moustache, and dark eyebrows made him look dreadful. He wore baggy trousers and heavy red-leather slippers with upturned toes, and he had a carbine slung over his back. He was a Pathan. The Pathans, an Afghan ethnic group, are war-riors who obey neither God nor man. Their law is the law of the rifle and the knife. He told us that he could take only three or four people at a time. My parents decided that I should go with my aunt and uncle.

We had to dress like the Pathan peasants who lived near 16 the border, so that our western clothes did not advertise the fact that we were from the capital and trying to escape. My uncle dressed like the Smuggler. My aunt and I were given dresses with colorful patterns and sequins (which made the dresses very heavy) and dangling jewelry. In addition, outside the city, the women were obliged to wear a Chaderi, a veil through which we could see but not be seen. It comes in three colors: yellowish-brown, gray, and blue. Ours were yellowish-brown.

We left the house at dawn and walked a mile or two to 17 reach the main road. While walking, the Chaderi twisted and clung to my legs. As I looked down to unwrap it, I stumbled over a rock and fell to the ground, injuring my right knee slightly. It burned, but I managed to catch up with my aunt and uncle and acted like nothing had happened. After a short time, a lorry arrived for us, and we spent the next few hours with sheep and goats, covering our faces with a piece of cloth to keep the smell and the dust out.

The sound of a helicopter approaching got our attention. 18 It was an MI-24, a kind of armored helicopter that the Russians used to bombard villages, agricultural fields, and mosques. We feared that this time we might be its target, but fortunately it passed us. After a few minutes, we came upon a village. From a small opening in the side of the lorry, I witnessed the after-

math of a bombardment. The air attack had reduced the village to rubble, and those who survived it were running around
shouting and screaming. An agricultural field outside the village was burned to ashes, and a pall of smoke and dust drifted
over the valley. The images of those people and their ruined
village haunted us the rest of our journey.

After a few hours the lorry stopped, and the driver opened   19
the gate and called, "Last stop." Holding the Chaderi, I jumped
to the ground. The desert was covered with the tracks of
horses, donkeys, camels, and people. There were many groups
of people travelling in caravans: young orphaned boys; a
lonely man with a sad expression on his face, all of his posses-
sions packed on top of a camel; and numerous donkeys carrying women while their husbands walked alongside. We were all
on our way to Pakistan.

As we waited for our donkeys, my uncle whispered to me: 20
"The Smuggler is a government agent, a Militia." My heart
skipped a beat. I knew exactly what that meant — he would turn
us in. The government recruits tribesmen like the Smuggler
for undercover assignments. The Smuggler was talking with
some other people, looking at us as he spoke. When he started
to walk toward us, I thought my life was over. I wanted to scream
and run. He stopped and signaled my uncle to come. As they
walked toward a mud hut in the distance, my whole life flashed
in front of my eyes. I saw my school, my parents, my execution.

"Did they take him for interrogation?" I asked myself. I   21
could see the hut, and I wondered what was going on inside.
When my uncle came out the door, I ran to him. He had been
bargaining for the price of the mules. We rented four mules
and set out with the caravan.

Riding that mule was an experience that I will never forget.   22
It was hard to stay balanced with the heavy dress and the veil,
especially once we began to climb a mountain. The trail was
just wide enough for the mule to put down his hooves. As we
turned and twisted along the mountainside, I wondered
whether I should close my eyes, to try to shut out the danger, or
keep them open, to be prepared when we fell down the side of
the mountain. But the mule was surefooted and I didn't fall. I
learned that if I could relax, I would not fall off.

It was a hot summer day, and I became thirsty. The sun was   23
right above our heads, and my thirst became intolerable. My
mouth was completely dry. We could see a village at the bottom
of the mountain — four hours away, according to the Smuggler.
After a few minutes, however, we got to a small lake. The water
was yellow and covered with algae, but the Smuggler drank it
and brought me a cup of water to drink. As I looked into the
cup, I was reminded of the solution that we prepared in biol-
ogy class in order to grow bacteria. This was the main source
of water for the village. God knows what microorganisms were
swimming in that lake.

"I wouldn't drink it if I were you," my aunt said.   24

But I closed my eyes, and drank the whole cup at once. I   25
would worry about the consequences later.

We reached the village just before sunset. After eating din-   26
ner and resting for several hours, we started to travel again.
The night journey was magnificent. The sky was clear, the
moon was full, and millions of stars seemed to be winking
at the night travelers. We could hear the bells of another caravan coming from the opposite direction, getting louder and
louder as it got close. The ding-a-ling of that caravan added a
rhythm to the lonely desert.

Now we were in the territory of the Freedom Fighters. We   27
knew if they recognized the Smuggler, they would execute all
of us as communist spies. The Freedom Fighters and the
Militia are enemies, and the Freedom Fighters did not trust
anyone who was travelling with an agent.

At dawn we reached a small tea house. It consisted of a   28
large bare room with a dirt floor covered by canvas mats. A few
small windows, with plastic in place of glass, let in a bit of light.
A smoky wood fire in a tin stove served for heating and boiling
water for tea. The owner brought us tea and bread, a soothing
sight for restless travelers.

We walked on, and soon a sign post got my attention. As I   29
got closer, I was able to read the words:

"WELCOME TO PAKISTAN."   30

I started to cry, walking backwards to get one last glimpse   31
of my beloved country.

· Chapter 3 ·

Remembering People

The four essays in this chapter demonstrate an important point about portraits of remembered people: it's possible to be appreciative without being sentimental. Even in those essays which focus on the writer's relationship with the person portrayed, the writers seem to present themselves as "characters" in their own stories, thus maintaining an emotional distance between themselves and their subjects.

In addition to this common strength, each of these essays has individual strengths. Although Larry Wooley and Cheri Mahan each tie the incidents of their narratives together with a subtle unifying theme, they handle them quite differently. In Mahan's essay, the thematic device is a piece of folded aluminum foil, both the first and last image we encounter in the essay. In Wooley's essay the theme emerges and develops gradually as the essay progresses.

Erick Young uses descriptive detail beautifully to capture the personality of his former teacher, eschewing long passages of dialogue in favor of occasional snatches of her speech — just enough to reveal her humor and individual style. And Dawn Sanders, writing insightfully about a childhood acquaintance she knew only slightly, shows us that the most significant people in our lives need not be those closest to us.

To LaVerne

. . .

Cheri L. Mahan

Blinn College
Brenham, Texas

Over the years, everyone in my family teased my mother-in-law about something we, typical yuppies of the eighties, considered a ridiculous habit. She saves used tinfoil. When cleaning up after big family meals, we would make smart remarks and roll our eyes heavenward as LaVerne gathered up and washed the used tinfoil. She would always reply good-naturedly: "You never know when you're going to need a good piece of foil!" With my carefree limited knowledge of poverty, I did not realize how deeply the concept of thrift can be instilled in the mind of someone raised during the Great Depression. Daily life in those difficult times revolved around the old saying "waste not, want not." 1

LaVerne was the second of four children born to Jessica and Mac McCain in a small, dust-blown town in Texas. She always had a certain pride in being from Olney, Texas. Her father was a mechanic for Ford Motor Company, and her mother delighted in taking care of her children and home. 2

Their small, wood-framed house was always immaculate. The furniture consisted of odds and ends accumulated over the years, but Jessica cared for it tenderly. Each Saturday morning, she waxed the wooden floors until they gleamed. She crocheted white lace doilies to cover the threadbare arms of 3

22

the upholstered chairs, and made cushions of bright, floral prints to liven up the room. The gleaming, dust-free library table held the family's prized possession: a radio.

The garden provided plenty of vegetables, especially beans 4 and potatoes, to satisfy the ever-increasing appetites of four growing children. When needy neighbors were reduced to eating only water gravy, the beans and potatoes were gladly shared. When the soles of their shoes got holes in them, the McCains employed a little southern ingenuity and made cardboard inserts. Dresses made of flour sacks were worn proudly and appreciated more than the "Better Wear" we get today from Foleys. Though there were few frills, the bare necessities were meagerly met with grateful hearts. By their examples, Mac and Jessica cheerfully taught LaVerne that economy is the art of making the most of life. It was a lesson well learned.

After the Depression, times were still very hard for the 5 McCains. Their account at the grocery store was never completely paid off before new charges were added. At twelve years of age, LaVerne had already reached her adult height of five feet, eight inches, and one day, as she dressed for school, nothing seemed to fit. Her long arms and even longer legs were too long for her well-worn clothes. "I don't have a thing to wear!" she complained to her mother. That afternoon, she found not one, but two, new dresses her mother had sewn for her that day. One of the dresses was made from a piece of fabric her mother had long been saving for herself. To this day, the guilt of a thoughtless, though innocent, remark made as a child, weighs heavy on LaVerne's heart.

LaVerne was fourteen years old when she went to work sell- 6 ing tickets at the picture show. From that time on, she was always self-sufficient. Never did she demand money from her parents for the school band trip, or for a cap and gown for high school graduation ceremonies. The money she earned was not spent on the latest rock video or gasoline for "cruisin'," but on school supplies and shoes. Even as a teenager, she knew that "to waste not" was "to want not."

Later on, as a young wife and mother, she applied the 7 lessons from her childhood. All leftovers were saved. Even a tablespoon of green beans she could use again in some way.

The toothpaste tube could be cut open, to find a week's supply of toothpaste left on the sides. One small, twenty-five foot roll of tinfoil could last at least a year. Those lean years developed an inner consciousness that quietly whispered with every flip of the pocketbook, "Waste not, want not!"

Through the years, LaVerne and her husband have been able to obtain and maintain a middle-class standard of living. They own a comfortable brick home, complete with a German shepherd and an automatic garage-door opener. However, as she nears retirement age, the old lessons tug even stronger on the strings of her conscience. Even with conserving, will there be enough money to meet all her needs? 8

I would love to reassure her that her needs will always be met. As long as I have hands to work, this precious mother-by-choice will never go without. Her quick wit, loving spirit, and contagious laugh are characteristics I have imitated. I seem to have imitated her in other ways, as well, and I think of her fondly when I open my kitchen drawer and reach for the neatly folded, used tinfoil. 9

Ken

■　■　■

Larry Wooley

Eastern Michigan University
Ypsilanti, Michigan

The stars shone brightly on that balmy summer night. Ken 1
and I were lying on our backs in the grass in his backyard. The
fire we had built nearby made shadows dance across the lawn.
We were near the shore of the lake, and the rising half moon
illuminated the waves as they lapped gently at the pontoons of
Ken's boat. Our conversation was sparse, but we didn't need to
say much. We were close friends reflecting on the past and also
dreaming about the future.

"Ken?" 2

"Yeah," he replied in a nonchalant tone of voice. 3

"What do you think college is going to be like?" 4

"I don't know. Are you scared?" 5

I covered up quickly, "No. . . . Well, maybe a little, but it's 6
still two years away."

"What do you want to be?" Ken asked. 7

"I was thinking of maybe being a psychiatrist. How about 8
you?"

"I don't know," he replied. That was typical of Ken. He 9
never thought much about the future, pretty much living life
from day to day. "Something that pays enough for me to buy a
DeLorean," he said in another typical Ken-like afterthought.

We rambled through some memories, and soon college 10
crept up again.

"Lare, where have you thought about going to college?" 11

"Wherever someone will give me a scholarship," I answered. 12

"You'll get one with your grades. I've been thinking about 13
Evangel myself." Evangel was in Missouri, and it was where
Karleen, his oldest sister, went to school. Then it hit me—we
weren't going to be inseparable forever.

"Ken, do you think we'll still be close by our first class 14
reunion?"

"Of course, Lare!" he answered too quickly. "We won't lose 15
touch. Time won't change anything." He didn't sound convinced, and I knew he was thinking the same thing that I was.

The fire grew dim, and we packed up. I went to my home, 16
just across the street.

Ken and I have known each other since seventh grade. I 17
was quiet and studious; Ken was a show-off. He was magnetic,
with an appealing sense of humor and great charm. Girls
were drawn to his looks. Ken was tall and thin, and he saun-
tered comfortably, taking large strides and swinging his arms
rather carelessly. Some would say he swaggered. His eyes were
shiny and so dark they were almost black. If you looked close,
there was always a light dancing behind them somewhere,
promising mischief if you stayed around. He had a light-
hearted smirk.

Ken's mother was a beautician, and she always made sure 18
that his brown hair was styled perfectly. That is, except for one
unruly cowlick she couldn't get rid of. It hung above his eyes,
giving the finishing touches to his jester-like appearance. We
had very little in common. But in a way our differences bonded
our friendship even more for we both admired the other's qualities. I can still remember the day I became his friend.

It was a cool fall afternoon when I was thirteen. While 19
raking leaves I saw Ken come out of his house with his football
uniform on. He played in the junior league. As he waited for his
ride he meandered into my yard.

"Going to practice?" I asked. 20

"Yeah, I don't want to though." 21

"I wish I played. It seems like fun," I said, trying to gain   22
points with him.

"It isn't. The practices are awful, and the coach is a jerk," he   23
replied unhappily. "I'd rather stay at home and shoot baskets."
Ken was a basketball nut.

His ride was coming over the hill. As he walked to the road   24
he turned around.

"Hey, when I get back you wanna come over and shoot a few?"   25

I was flabbergasted. Mr. Popularity was asking me to do   26
something. "Well, I'm not that good," my weak voice replied.

"Who cares! I'll see you when I get back, Lare!" he said,   27
jumping into the van.

Lare? That sounded funny. No one had ever called me that   28
before. But I got used to it fast. By the end of high school I was
called nothing else.

We were always together. Many days we would purposely   29
miss the school bus home and go to the local arcade. We spent
our summers swimming and fishing. It was as if we came
straight from the pages of *Tom Sawyer*.

In junior high we even joined Youth Involvement because   30
every other member was female. I actually got out and met people when I was around Ken! And when he had troubles with his
school work I'd help him out. During study sessions at his dining room table, his mother used to walk back and forth saying,
"Ken would get better grades if he would just pay attention."
She was right. Ken was bright, but he'd rather be having fun.

Slowly, the differences between us began to melt. You   31
could say we rubbed off on each other. Each complemented
the other in a friendship that was remarkably equal. Neither of
us dominated, and we also respected each other's opinions.

It was during our freshman year of high school that I first   32
noticed some of Ken's attributes in myself. He approached one
day with a sign in his hand. It read

First Annual
SLH Air Jam!
Lip-Sync Competition
Tryouts Monday

I'd heard about it. South Lyon High was seeking volunteers to perform lip-sync routines at a special assembly.

"Ohh Ken," I groaned. "No. We can't. We're just freshmen.   33
They'll kill us! Ken, I won't." And as he sat there grinning, I knew I was in fact going to do this. Ken picked the song, and we practiced for two weeks. When the dreaded day finally arrived, our group of five was scheduled to go last, fit for the killing. We were the only freshman group; all the others were seniors. The crowd was tough, and gave the other acts only moderate applause for their rock-song routines. In fact, the assembly seemed pretty lame.

When we heard our introduction, we came out of the   34
locker room — four puny freshmen dressed like Egyptians, car-rying Ken on a litter. For just one second the crowd was silent. Then a roaring wave of laughter and cheers hit as Ken, dressed as a pharaoh, jumped down to the tune of Steve Martin's "King Tut." The routine lasted only three minutes, during which time I felt weak and dizzy, but exhilarated. It was the most glorious three minutes of my life. We were a hit. We exited to a standing ovation. The crowd continued to cheer, chanting "Tut, Tut, Tut." We came out and took a bow. "King Tut" had won, unani-mously. In that short period of time I had emerged from my shell, thanks to two years of Ken's role modeling and his con-stant pressure to participate in the Air Jam. It had been fun! It was wonderful being in front of those people looking like a fool. We brought the house down while also establishing a tra-dition. Every year afterwards our group did some outrageous act for the Air Jam. We became legends.

My influence on Ken was more subtle. He was beginning to   35
slow down and take more time out for his schoolwork. He wasn't jumping from girlfriend to girlfriend like he once did. The change became noticeable to all in our senior year. He set-tled down with one quiet girl, Elaine, whom he's been with for over a year. Ken also realized what he wanted to do with his life. We had D. Jayed dances throughout high school and it directed him toward the area of broadcasting. Ken enrolled at Spec Howard's School of Broadcasting in his senior year. Graduat-ing second in his class, Ken became the first student to ever attend while still in high school. I persuaded him to enter a

contest for producing amateur commercials dealing with drug abuse. From over five hundred entries statewide, many made collectively by high school classes, Ken's won. They were later aired locally on the major television networks. Ken had applied himself, and he succeeded.

We don't see each other very often now. I'm living at EMU, 36 and he's at home, going to OCC and working. We really began to drift apart in our senior year. Both of us sensed it, and in my yearbook he wrote,

> Dear King (Tut) Larry,
>
> I'm sure you'll agree our venture in high school has been an interesting one. And I'll never regret a moment. Even though our schedules have changed, our friendship hasn't — and it won't. Take it easy Lare.
>
> Ken

I wonder if he knows the 8 × 10 of us at the Summit, taken 37 the night he was on the King's Court, hangs above my desk? Or that my fondest memories of childhood were the long summer days we spent together. It doesn't matter. I've seen him only five times since I began college, but each time it was as if nothing had changed. Ken was right. We're still great friends, and we always will be.

Only She

• • •

Erick Young

University of California at San Diego
La Jolla, California

Those eyes. Brown. No no, deep, dark brown. Hardly a wrinkle around them. Soft, smooth skin. And those eyebrows. Neither thick nor thin, just bold — two curves punctuating her facial expressions with a certain something. Surprise, amusement — up would shoot one of the brows, the right one I believe, just slightly, accompanied by a mischievous little smirk. Anger, irritation — up and inward shot both brows, tightly pressed, followed by a sharp "What d'ya want? Don't bother me!" She never really meant it, though; it was just her way of saying hello. Even though she wore glasses she could still see all, with or without them. Her deep, dark brown eyes were no ordinary eyes; no, within those deep wells rested a pair of magic orbs, two miniature crystal balls that could peer into your mind and read all your little thoughts. Some thought she had psychic powers. She knew what you were thinking, or at least she always seemed to know what I was thinking, even my most complex, inexplicable thoughts. And that was all that seemed to matter at the time. Only she, only Sonia Koujakian, Mrs. K.

I do not recall the first time I noticed her at school, but Mrs. K was not one to blend into a crowd. I would see her walking briskly across the school rotunda, tall and lean, wearing a skirt and a mauve-colored raincoat, holding a stuffed beige handbag in one hand, and a bright red coffee pot in the other. She seemed so confident, always looking straight ahead as she walked about school. Perhaps it was her hair that first caught my eye. It was short, a mix of light brown and gray, combed slightly up—almost spiked. Not the typical sort of hairstyle for an English teacher at our school. It set her apart and made her look dynamic. Already I knew that she was somebody special.

The PSAT brought her into my life for the first time, in my 3 sophomore year. Even though she was the senior English teacher, she offered to coach any undaunted sophomores or juniors after school for the nefarious "SAT jr." Trying to be the savvy student, I joined a small group who gathered in her cove after school to practice vocabulary drills and sentence completions. Mrs. K would scold us on the finer points of grammar, giving us her "come on, get with the production" look as we reviewed our errors. Not the typical reaction from a teacher; she treated us like peers, and would say to us whatever was on her mind without pretense, pleasantry, or euphemism. We could do the same, if we had the guts to try. Her casual disposition made me feel both relaxed and nervous; none of us knew how to act around her, whether to joke and tease her, or respect and honor her. We all agreed, however, that she was as down-to-earth as they come. Two years later, as an older and wiser senior, I would get a full dose of Mrs. K's personality.

My first day in Mrs. K's class left much to be desired. I 4 entered to find most of my classmates just laughing and joking. The first-day-of-school jitters had become passé, and the smugness that comes with seniordom dominated the room. It was a convention of Alfred E. Neumans, and the nonchalant air of "What Me Worry?" filled the classroom. Some students, however, sat very quietly. These were the wise ones, they'd heard about Mrs. K. Academic tensions hovered like the inevitable black storm cloud above Room 5C3. There was a small fear of the unknown and the unexpected nudging about in my stomach as I sat at the far end of the center table. Strange how this was the only classroom in the entire building to have six huge wooden tables instead of forty individual little desks; someone must have wanted it that way. For once I was not too anxious to sit up front. Suddenly the chattering diminished. Mrs. K was coming.

31

In she ambled, with her stuffed handbag and bright red 5
coffee pot, wearing a skirt and the mauve raincoat; she was just
as I had remembered. She scanned the room, and up went her
right eyebrow. A most peculiar "I-know-what-you-are-up-to"
smirk was our first greeting. Now I was nervous.

"All right ladies and gentlemen, I want to see if you belong 6
in my class," she began. "Take out a pen and lots of paper."
Pause. "Now don't get too worried over this, since you are all
geniuses anyway. You know, if you've got it you've got it, if you
don't. . . ." She shrugged. Pause. "Some of you know you don't
really belong in here," she chided, pointing her finger, "and it's
time you stopped getting put in Honors English just because
you passed some silly little test in second grade. Well now we're
going to see what you can do. Okay now, stop and think for a
moment, and get those creative juices going. I want you to
write me a paper telling me the origin of the English language.
You can be as creative as you want. Make up something if you
have to — two cavemen grunting at each other, I don't care. You
have until the end of the period. Go."

It was not the most encouraging welcome. For a moment 7
the whole class just sort of slumped in their seats, drained suddenly of all vitality and hopes of a relaxed senior year. Blank
faces abounded, mine included. I had no idea what to write.
The origin of the English language? Being "creative" seemed
too risky. What ever happened to the good ol' five paragraph
essay with specific examples? Well I didn't have any specific
examples anyway. I remember staring at a sheet of white paper,
then scrawling down some incoherent mumbo-jumbo. I wanted
to impress her, too much. "It was nice knowing you," I sighed as
I handed in my paper. What a first day.

Fortunately, that first day with Mrs. K would not be my last. 8
Although the class size shrunk the following days as some stu-
dents ran for their academic lives, I was not prepared to leave.
I knew Mrs. K's class would be an arduous English journey, but
I could never let myself miss it. It would be a journey well worth
taking.

As the weeks continued, tidbits of Mrs. K's colorful past 9
and philosophy about life would somehow always creep into
lectures and class discussions. We found out she had served as

a volunteer nurse in a combat hospital in Japan and had "seen it all—even grown men cry." During the 60s a wilder Mrs. K could be seen cruising the streets of San Francisco on motorcycle, decked out in long spiked boots and short spiked hair. She later traded in her motorcycle and boots for a Fiat and white Reeboks. And there was a running joke about her age. Mrs. K could not be much less that 45, but just as Jack Benny was forever 49, she was forever 28. One of her T-shirts said so. Twenty-eight was a good year, she would tell us, but she never quite explained why.

I would come to deeply trust and respect this eccentric   10
lady. I guess I have Oedipus Rex to thank for our first class meeting. We had to compose an extensive essay on the Oedipus Trilogy, on which much of our semester grade would be based. Foolishly, I chose to write on the most abstract topic, predestination and divine justice. I toiled for days, torturing myself trying to come up with some definitive conclusions. Finally, I realized my struggle was merely carrying my mind farther and farther adrift in a sea of confusion. I needed someone to rescue me; I needed Mrs. K.

We arranged to meet in the Faculty Commons, a small,   11
smoky room of teachers with red pens at work and administrators shooting the breeze over lunch. I crept inside with notes in hand and took a seat. She soon arrived, holding a tuna-on-wheat, a chocolate chip cookie, and the red coffee pot. "I hope you don't mind if I eat while we talk," she said, "but if you do, I'm going to eat anyway." Smile.

We talked the whole lunch period. I felt awkward at first,   12
actually struggling to explain why I'd been struggling with the assignment. But then Mrs. K the Mentor emerged—soft spoken, introspective, wise. I opened up to her. We sat beside each other at that table, reflecting on predestination, divine justice, and life. A ray of sunshine cut through clouds of confusion. Our reflections were interrupted by the lunch bell, but we continued later after school. Two days and two drafts later, I had gained more than just a deep understanding of Oedipus Rex: I had gained a friend. What was it about this woman that enabled me to reveal a different part of myself? Never before had I spoken so openly about my thoughts, or about myself.

Most people did not understand my cares and thoughts. But she understood.

I would go back to Room 5C3 many afternoons later to sort   13
my thoughts. To her I was no longer Erick but Hamlet, because of my pensive and complex nature. "Okay Hamlet, what's on your mind?" our conversations would begin. Every writing assignment became an excuse to spend time after school talking and reflecting, me at the wooden table, her at her stool. We digressed on everything from Paradise Lost to Shakespeare to "The Road Not Taken." Sometimes other students would come for help on their papers, and I would always let them go first, so that I could be the last left. Often I would learn about more than just literature: "Life's not black and white, it's a hazy gray, and you've always got to use that wonderful piece of machinery God gave you and question things because nothing is clear-cut." I noticed my perceptions changing, as well as my writing style. More of my character entered my writing, and the Mr. Detached Impartiality persona I once favored faded into the background. Being "creative" no longer seemed risky. She told me to put more of myself into my creations, and I listened.

One afternoon near the end of my senior year, I asked her   14
about her favorite novel. "Oh, without a doubt, *Les Miserables*," she replied. "But I never could find an unedited version." On Graduation Day, in a sea of seniors hugging one another, red and blue mortarboards sailing through the air, I searched through the crowd for Mrs K and handed her a small box. Inside with a long thank-you on the cover was a new copy of *Les Miserables*, unedited and unabridged.

I doubt that I will come across many others like Mrs. K.   15
Only she would sit with me one-on-one, and review every minute detail of a draft. Only she would give up an afternoon just to shoot the breeze. Only she could I call a mentor, a confidant, and a friend. I still think of Mrs. K. Sometimes, when the pressures of college come crashing down, and the order of life seems to have run amok, I go to my room and slowly close the door and my eyes, sit down, and talk with Mrs. K.

"Okay Hamlet, what's on your mind. . . ."   16

Beth

■　■　■

Dawn Sanders

University of North Dakota
Grand Forks, North Dakota

I used to see her walking alone in the crowded hallways. 1
Sometimes a group of girls would follow behind whispering
and giggling after her. Occasionally, boys would tease. Our eyes
met once, but her gaze fell quickly to the floor, as if in shame.
If she only knew that it was I, not she, who should have felt
ashamed.

Beth did not graduate with my grade-school class, but we 2
had been classmates through seventh grade. As I look back, I
realize that those were the best years of my childhood, unbur-
dened with cares and responsibilities. But even carefree, innocent children can be cruel.

From the very beginning, Beth was different, an outsider. 3
Her physical appearance set her apart. Stringy blond hair
framed her homely face and accentuated her long pointy nose.
She had a bad overbite, probably caused by her incessant
thumb-sucking. On her bony shoulders hung an old, faded
sweater, out of shape from too many washings, and hopelessly
out of style. With her sallow complexion, she looked mal-
nourished. We all thought she was dense. The ideas that were
easy for us to understand seemed out of her reach. She
remained at the bottom of the class, never seeming to benefit
from the teacher's help.

We excluded Beth from our games. If we did let her join, it 4
was so we could gang up and laugh at her. The boys all called
her names, pulling her hair and stealing her food at lunch. At
first, Beth fought back, but after a time she seemed to lose
spirit. She became quiet and withdrawn.

I remember one incident in particular. It was in the fifth 5
grade. The class bully, Fred Washek, was also the teacher's son.
Fred did whatever he wanted to do, which was normally something cruel. During Fred's reign of terror, Beth was his main
target. He taunted and tormented her.

One day, while Mrs. Washek was running an errand, Fred 6
put a tack on Beth's chair. I don't know if she noticed it, but she
hesitated to sit down. Fred commanded her to sit and threatened to knock her down if she disobeyed. Beth refused. Fred
pushed her hard into the chair. Immediately, she jumped up,
wincing in pain. Fred angrily pushed her down again and held
her there. The class had been enjoying Fred's prank but
became increasingly uneasy. Still, no one dared come to Beth's
defense for fear of Fred's vengeance. Finally, the teacher
returned and Fred calmly went back to his seat. In the meantime, Beth began to whimper. Mrs. Washek ignored her as
usual, but as Beth's sobs became louder, she scolded her for
being a cry baby and disturbing the class.

That incident made me realize how terribly we all had been 7
treating Beth. When the others teased her, I no longer joined in.
But I did nothing to stop them. Nor did I become her friend.
The term was nearly over by then and Beth's grades were so
poor that she was held back. She was probably happy to get
away from us. I think I was a little relieved to get away from her.

Her being held back turned out to be the best thing for 8
her. The class she moved into was more accepting. I saw her
now and then over the next five years and saw her make friends
and gain confidence. Her grades improved. She joined the var-
sity volleyball team and became assistant librarian. She got a
part-time job and was able to get some stylish clothes.

I came more and more to admire Beth. She cast off the 9
label of loser that our class had given her and made something
of herself. In fact, she always had been special; we just never
noticed. We saw only the shell, not the person within.

• Chapter 4 •

Writing Profiles

Essentially journalistic in nature, the profile draws on a variety of techniques from both print and electronic media. Melanie Papenfuss's "Behind the Sugar Curtain" is a case in point. Written in a class that used *The New Yorker* as a supplementary text, is reminiscent of certain "behind the scenes" features in that magazine. And yet some of its techniques — the present tense narrative, the dialogue format, the dramatic evocation of scene — bring to mind live television reporting as well.

Although Al Cronin's technique is quite different from Papenfuss's — no quotes, just description — the detail in hi profile of the Yale Bologna Festival is so sharp that, once again, we may feel we're right there on the scene, filming the coronation of the King and Queen of Bologna. Pervading Cronin's essay is a touch of irony so subtle we're never quite sure it's intended. Is he playing it straight when he's describing those outhouse races, or do we detect an ever-so-slight wink of the eye?

The other three writers combine the techniques of the first two blending interview, observation, and background material into coherent, well-structured human interest features. Making good use of direct quotation, Diane Schaeffer and Katy Reising capture the personalities of their interview subjects, a child psychologist and a spunky grocery store cashier. In her profile of a small town bagel bakery, Colleen Starkey uses sensory details to invoke not only the sight and smell but even the

37

taste of bagels fresh from the oven. In all three pieces, it's as if the writer is well-tuned to the reader's needs and interests, switching modes at crucial moments to keep us reading.

In the *St. Martin's Guide*, we are told that profiles "center on a theme that nearly always reveals surprise or contrast in the subject or in the writer's response to it." That "surprise" element of behind-the-scenes stories like Papenfuss's is always apparent, but it is less obvious in the other essays. What *does* account for the "human interest" factor in these essays? This is a subject that might be worth some discussion.

Behind the Sugar Curtain

■   ■   ■

Melanie Papenfuss

University of North Dakota
Grand Forks, North Dakota

Ten-thirty on a Friday night I pull into my cousin Blaine's   1
farmyard. The old white two-story house is dark. I grab my
overnight bag from the backseat and quickly make my way into
the house. Silence. I know Blaine is home: his pick-up is in
the driveway. I flick on the kitchen light and look around.
What a mess!

During beet season, which runs from the first week in   2
October until all the beets are out of the ground, I expect the
house to be messy, but nothing like this. A red and white cooler
is sitting on the table, half open. Through the crack I can see
empty sandwich bags, two cans of Coke, and an empty bag of
Ruffles potato chips. On the counter sits a box of Wheaties and
a carton of milk, still waiting to be put away. Dishes are piled
high in the sink. My eyes wander to the living room. The hide-
a-bed is laying out, obviously being used regularly. Dirty laun-
dry is scattered about.

"Melanie, is that you?"   3

From the bedroom, Blaine walks out, wearing a pair of old   4
basketball shorts. Dark brown hair, matted on one side of his
head and sticking out on the other, sleepy eyes, and a groggy
voice materialize before my eyes.

"You're just getting up?" I stare in disbelief.   5

39

"Ya," he replies while rubbing the sleep from his eyes. "I 6
work at night and sleep by day. I am lucky enough to have been
given the night shift rather than the day." As an afterthought he
looks at what he is wearing, or not wearing. "Let me get
dressed."

He returns with a red turtleneck, red and black flannel 7
shirt, and faded Wrangler jeans.

"My shift starts at midnight, but I like to be in the field by 8
11:30." The left side of his upper lip curls into a cocky smirk.
"Do you think you can handle an all-nighter?"

Before I can answer he continues. "What do you want to 9
bring to eat—sandwiches, chips, cookies, Rice Krispie bars,
Coke, Pepsi, Dr. Pepper?"

"I thought this was for twelve hours, not twelve days!" I sim- 10
ply shrug, "Pack what you like."

Quickly he throws together four salami and cheese sand- 11
wiches, a bag of chips, some Rice Krispie bars, and a six-pack
of Coke. After the food supply is safely tucked away, we go into
the living room to catch a weather report.

The announcer blasts, "For all you farmers, you can expect 12
clear skies. Those stars will shine tonight!"

Blaine jumps out of his chair and flicks the TV off. "That's 13
all I needed to hear. Let's go."

He grabs the cooler and his red St. Thomas Standard jacket 14
and walks out the door. I shut off the lights and quickly follow.

We reach the field at 11:15 P.M. All I can see from the road 15
is a large light emanating from the middle of the field. I look
closer, and alongside the bright light I can see orange parking
lights suspended in mid-air. Blaine turns into the field and
heads toward the light.

A gruff voice comes from the CB. "Blaine, is that you?" 16

"Ya, John, and I have a passenger tonight. You remember 17
Melanie, don't ya?" Blaine looks at me and winks.

"I sure do," John replies with a chuckle. A large older man 18
with silver hair and wire-rimmed glasses, John is the owner of
all the beets. "Kevin should be back with the truck in about
fifteen minutes. You can take over then."

We pass the machine producing the light. It is a 4440 John 19
Deere tractor with four headlights. Behind it a weird looking

40

contraption is being pulled. It looks like a plow or cultivator but with a long armlike structure that rises up and disappears into the box.

"What is that thing behind the tractor?" 20

Blaine laughs, "That 'thing' is the beet lifter. It pulls the 21 beets up and into the truck box."

"Oh." 22

We reach the other side of the field, and Blaine stops the 23 pick-up. I turn and watch the beetlifter inch its way across the field. It reminds me of a snail creeping up and down the glass of a fish tank.

It's not long before I see headlights coming from the north. 24 It is Kevin's truck. He turns into the field, comes halfway in and stops. I am confused. Patiently I wait for him to continue toward us, but he doesn't. Instead I see his box begin to lift slowly into the air.

"What is he doing?" 25

"Do you mean Kevin?" Eagerly I nod yes. "He's dumping the 26 leftover dirt." Blaine shifts his body toward me and focuses his attention on my question. "You see, after you unload your beets at the plant, the dirt and beets are separated by the grab rollers and you get your dirt back. So then you put it back in the field it came from."

As Kevin drives toward us, Blaine grabs the cooler and tilts 27 his head in the direction of the truck. "That's where we're spending the night, so take everything you need."

The beet truck is a yellow and brown Mack truck. To get 28 into the cab I have to step onto a runner that is a foot and a half off the ground. There is even a handle on the left side that is perpendicular to the ground. The inside of the cab is small. There are two seats that squeak as you sit down. Between the seats is a cubbyhole for storage. On the steering wheel is a stainless steel knob to help the driver turn.

Blaine turns the radio on to KFGO, a country station. 29 "Jason's truck is full; that means we take over."

Jason, I think, must be the other driver. Blaine pushes in 30 the clutch and grinds the gears into first. The truck jerks to a slow start. Carefully Blaine pulls the truck box underneath the lifter and CBs to John to tell him we're ready.

Before long I hear the thudding of the beets in the empty 31
box. "How do you know when to pull forward or move back to
allow the beets to fill the truck evenly?"

"Do you see those arrows?" Blaine says, pointing out his 32
window to a panel of orange arrows attached to the tractor.
"When I need to speed up or slow down, John flicks a switch
and the appropriate arrow lights up."

"Oh." 33

After a few rounds (a round is one row of beets that runs 34
the entire length of the field), the truck is loaded. Now we head
north on the small country road for a mile until we reach a
paved road. There we turn east. It's twelve miles to the Crystal
Sugar Beet Plant in Drayton, North Dakota.

"How fast do you go?" 35

"With a full load I don't like to go over fifty. Empty I will go 36
sixty to sixty-five."

On the road to the plant we meet many empty trucks. 37
Blaine can tell me who was driving and where they are heading
by seeing only the headlights and the color of the truck.

After twenty minutes we reach the road that will take us to 38
the plant. We get in line with a few other trucks. Their boxes
are heaping with beets.

"Is our truck heaping too?" 39

Amused, Blaine replies, "Yes." 40

"Why don't the beets fly off when you are going down the 41
highway?"

"Because each beet weighs five to ten pounds. They're too 42
heavy to fly off."

It takes only a few minutes to reach the scale house. When 43
we get up to the scale house window, Blaine rummages
through some index card-like metal plates and hands one to
the lady in the window. I hear a stamp, and she gives Blaine a
slip of paper.

"What did you just do? What's that metal thing?" 44

"This metal thing is a number plate," Blaine explains 45
patiently. "It is recorded by the scale house. The number tells
them who owns the beets in the truck and how heavy the truck
is when it's loaded."

I turn and look to see where we are going. We are driving 46
on a single-lane paved road, but at the end it branches out into
eight separate roads, spread out like the bristles of a broom. At
the end of each is an orange machine (the piler); trucks are
driving up onto them.

Again we wait behind other trucks. When it's our turn, a 47
man in a hardhat signals for us to pull ahead. Slowly Blaine
releases the clutch and drives the big truck onto the piler.
There are railings on each side of us and I don't think we'll fit,
but I am wrong. Behind the truck the ramp is being raised so
it is perpendicular to the ground. Then Blaine gets a signal
that tells him to back up so the truck box gate is against the
inclined ramp. When this is done, Blaine can then begin to
raise the truck bed and dump the beets. Once the beets are
dumped, the piler separates the excess dirt from the beets.
From there the beets go up a long conveyor belt and are piled
on many other beets. The dirt is brought to a type of holding
bin and is then dumped back into the truck after it comes off
the piler.

We make our way back up the broom bristle and head for 48
the scale house. Blaine hands the lady in the window the paper
with his loaded weight, and she stamps it with his empty
weight. We have been carrying 44,000 pounds of beets—
twenty-two tons!

"So, now you've seen what goes on during beet season. 49
What do you think?"

"I never knew all the things that go on," I said in amaze- 50
ment. "How many more loads will we get to do before your
shift is over?"

"Probably five or six more if we have no breakdowns. Do 51
you want to go home or keep going?"

"Are you kidding?" I reply eagerly. "Pass me a Coke, would 52
ya?"

The Great American Bologna Festival

■　■　■

Allen Cronin

Eastern Michigan University
Ypsilanti, Michigan

The day has finally arrived: the First Annual Yale Bologna 1
Festival is about to begin. Bologna has been processed in Yale,
Michigan, since 1906, and it has been the city's trademark
since 1939, when Harry and Leota Hudzinski started their
little factory. The whole town has been looking forward to the
festival with great expectations.

The festivities begin on Saturday morning at eight o'clock 2
with the sidewalk sales. All of the local businesses have their
most irresistible deals displayed on the sidewalk in front of
their stores. Salerno Shoes is offering a second pair of shoes
for a nickel. Williams' Department Store has marked everything down from twenty to fifty percent. Inside the stores
is more of the same, and the smart shoppers are there bright
and early, to make sure they don't miss a thing. It is quite
a scene: shoppers scurrying from store to store, carrying par-
cels and dragging children. And the sidewalk sales are just
the beginning.

At ten o'clock comes the pet parade. Only children are 3
allowed to enter, but everyone gathers around to watch. Many
of the pets are decked out in their Sunday best. A brown dachs-

hund trots by in a hand-knitted blue and white striped sweater, followed by a large black poodle with a red velvet ribbon. The most unusual pet is a black and white goat who sports an old straw hat. The winning entry is a little blond-haired girl and her white poodle. They wear matching pink sweaters and bows. As the pet parade ends, the aroma of freshly cooked bologna lures folks to one of the festival's most significant events: the bologna-eating contest.

Some of the biggest eaters in Yale have shown up for this 4 colossal battle, which takes place in front of the grocery store. Two long tables are set up opposite each other, eight contestants at each. In front of each anxious contestant are twenty rings of bologna, stacked like pyramids to a height of around two feet. The contestants have five minutes to devour as much bologna as they can. A rather rotund gentleman starts off quickly, shoveling bologna into his mouth so fast that his arms are a blur. Very soon, however, his stomach tells him he has had enough. A chubby boy gobbles up an impressive portion of bologna, but he is no match for the really big eaters. The champion turns out to be a tall lanky teenager, who claims victory after eating sixteen rings. His closest challenger put away a mere twelve. Now everyone has just enough time to get a bologna dog and cold drink before rushing to the next event: the outhouse races.

The outhouse races are open to anyone, but only busi- 5 nesses have entered. Each team has built an outhouse that will hold one rider and contain basic necessities such as toilet paper and a nice variety of magazines. Four other team members push or pull the outhouse, depending on team strategy. Two teams race in each heat.

Even though the population of Yale is less than two thou- 6 sand, well over four thousand line Main Street, which is closed for the event. The teams race down the block to a garbage can, maneuver around it, and race back. The Commercial and Savings Bank's entry, all women, is obviously the crowd's favorite; nevertheless, they bow out early. In the finals, Worton's I.G.A. is speeding toward victory when unexpectedly their outhouse flips over sideways. The Bricker Brothers, owners of the hardware store, sneak by to capture the title.

45

Finally comes the event everyone has been waiting for, the crowning of the King and Queen of Bologna. The voting has taken place during the month before the festival. Canisters for each nominee were placed throughout town, and people pledged a penny for each vote they cast. Chuck Gaidica, from Channel Four in Detroit, is on hand to crown the King and Queen. Harry Hudzinski, the sentimental favorite, and Rose Lawson are crowned King and Queen. A ring of bologna is set on top of their heads, and the Queen is presented with a bouquet of carnations. It is obvious how proud the King and Queen are from the ear-to-ear smiles on their faces.

The people of Yale wanted to show what bologna has meant to their town, and they had a fun time doing so. As the crowd begins to head out, it is evident what many of them are thinking; only 364 more days until the Second Annual Bologna Festival.

A Taste of New York City in Downtown Durham

■ ■ ■

Colleen Starkey

University of New Hampshire
Durham, New Hampshire

It is a chilly fall morning. Many of the cars on the road are covered with a thick, crisp frost—a sure sign that another cold New England winter is on its way. To brighten their early morning and take the chill out of this fall day, many of the drivers and their passengers will start the morning off with a piping hot cup of coffee and a fresh, warm bagel straight from the oven. Although bagels are not exactly a traditional New England breakfast, they have become a normal part of life for many people in southern New Hampshire ever since the Bagelry opened its doors six years ago. Set in the college town of Durham, New Hampshire, the Bagelry offers authentic New York-style bagels in an atmosphere much like that of the small coffee shops and cafes that line the streets of New York.

"This New York connection is no accident," said the Bagelry's owner, Warren Daniels. Having moved from the New York City borough of Queens to the southeastern section of New Hampshire, Warren and his wife, Elise, saw a market for the traditional bagel in an area where even bakeries are a rarity. With help from a bagel consultant in Ithaca, New York, they set out to bring bagels to New Hampshire. Their dream became a

47

reality on March 17, 1983, the day the Bagelry opened its doors. It wasn't long before their business was booming — and they now supply the campus dining halls, the Memorial Union pub, the Greek houses, and most supermarkets in the area.

A typical day at the Bagelry starts at four o'clock in the morning, when the first batch of bagels is prepared for what is known as the morning bake. While most people are still sound asleep, one of the five official bakers begins the task of preparing the dough. The baker starts with one hundred pounds of flour. Other ingredients include yeast, malt, and salt, but no preservatives, sugar, or fat. In fact, bagels are actually less fattening than other kinds of bread. 3

All the ingredients are blended together in an enormous horizontal mixer. Once the dough reaches the proper consistency, it is transferred to another contraption — creatively labeled the Bagel Machine — that actually makes and shapes each individual bagel. This machine measures out three-ounce pieces of dough, forms them into rings, and pushes them down a large metal chute onto a canvas conveyor belt. At this point, the baker puts the bagels in rows on large flat boards. When all bagels have been put on boards, the boards are stacked on portable racks and covered with cloth sheaths to allow the bagels to rise. 4

The first step in cooking the bagels is what makes them authentic New York style. Unlike the frozen bagels for sale in supermarkets, these bagels are boiled before they are baked, a step that gives an attractive gloss to the outside and a lighter, fluffier consistency to the inside. After being boiled for approximately one minute, the bagels are baked at 550°F for fifteen to twenty minutes. At this time the aroma of hot, fresh baked goods fills the Bagelry. You can smell the yeast of dough rising and the strong tang of garlic and onion bagels. 5

The Bagelry offers twelve varieties of bagels to choose from, ranging from the old standbys to one actually invented by the proprietors. (If by chance your favorite is sold out when you arrive, try later in the day, for there is an afternoon bake as well.) As you walk into the Bagelry, you can see all the types aligned in wire baskets. First comes halitosis heaven, Garlic and Onion; for the more mellow palate, there are Wheat, Egg, and Plain. 6

Rye, Pumpernickel, and Oat cater to the health-conscious customer, followed by Sesame, Poppyseed, and Salt. Cinnamon Raisin brings up the rear and offers something on the sugaryside for those with a sweet tooth. While Onion and Cinnamon Raisin seem to be the most popular, the Oatmeal bagel, created by Elise Daniels, has attracted a large following as well. "I enjoy experimenting a lot with ideas at home," she said. "I'm constantly investigating new cookbooks and possible recipes."

Elise is largely responsible for the Bagelry's enticing menu, which includes many variations on the basic bagel. Along with bagels by the dozen, you can get a bagel toasted, with cream cheese or assorted spreadables, or even done up like a sandwich.   7

Also available are fresh baked knishes — another New York specialty, consisting of dough with meat, cheese, and other fillings — as well as various quiches, breads, cakes, brownies, and delicious but fattening six-layer bars. In addition, you can indulge in hot or cold soups with a side order of bagel chips.   8

But along with its large, assorted menu of tasty treats, the Bagelry has something more to offer — atmosphere. It is a quiet, serene shop that is well lighted and comfortably decorated, with bright white walls and a clean appearance. The Bagelry serves a large number of people, yet it offers quiet spaces to converse with friends or read without distraction. You can slip back to a far corner, bagel and coffee in hand, and settle down with a complimentary national or local paper — or you can sit under hanging plants in the front enjoying the comforts of the indoors while gazing at the outdoors.   9

The relaxed atmosphere is very welcoming to the frazzled business executive and the "always-on-the-go" college student. Quite often, area businesspeople will hold informal interviews at the bagelry, and during finals time each semester, many students can be seen studying there. A majority of customers are regulars.   10

All in all, the Bagelry is a place for everyone to enjoy, pleasing all tastes from plain to adventurous, at all meals — breakast, lunch, and dinner. This restaurant/bakery boasts fast, accommodating, pleasant service. And it's the only one of its kind in this area of New England. So if ever you have a craving for an authentic New York bagel, the Bagelry can satisfy your desire.   11

49

Jan Winn: Child Therapist

. . .

Diane Schaeffer

University of California at San Diego
La Jolla, California

Sara was four years old. Her home was a storage shed that she shared with her two-year-old brother, new baby brother, mother, and her mother's boyfriend, who physically and sexually abused the children. Sara had the responsibility of caring for her siblings. In a heap on the floor was a huge pile of dirty diapers. The small, rundown shed had no plumbing. Bare mattresses were placed on the floor among the rats. A strong stench emanated from a refrigerator. 1

The therapists at the privately run Child Guidance Clinic, a part of Children's Hospital and Health Center, counsel many children like Sara. About thirty percent are abused. Others come because they have discipline problems; are aggressive or withdrawn; or need help resolving some other emotional, behavioral, or interpersonal problem. The children range from infant to age eighteen. About half of them are grade-school age and the other half are a mixture of teenagers and preschoolers. 2

Jan Winn, an energetic petite figure with shoulder-length brown hair, has been a therapist at the Child Guidance Clinic for seven years. She sees about four or five patients every day. For her, the work is both demanding and rewarding. "Sometimes you have to keep yourself from becoming frustrated and 3

angry," she says, her blue eyes sincere. "You have to remain distant enough to keep from being overwhelmed by the children's
problems. It is not easy for therapists to see children who have
been hurt, but it is satisfying to see the children begin to thrive
because of the therapy."

Jan tells about one of her patients Tina, a tall eleven-year-   4
old. On her first visit, after she and her father checked in with
the receptionist behind the glass window, she sat patiently
beside her father in the clinic's waiting room. Jan soon
appeared, cheerfully introduced herself, and invited Tina into
her office. Suddenly, Tina became sullen and refused to budge
from her chair, exclaiming, "No, I won't go!" No reasoning or
coaxing could persuade her to change her mind, so her father
scooped up his struggling, screaming daughter and carried
her into Jan's office, where he unceremoniously dumped her
into the arms of a chair and quickly left. Jan then tried unsuc-
cessfully to begin the session. "You can't make me stay," Tina
announced, heading toward the closed door. Jan reached out,
grabbed her by the waist, and pulled her onto her lap. "You
won't believe this," said Jan, shaking her head as she related the
episode. "Tina snuggled up, put her head on my shoulder, and
fell asleep."

Most of the time, Jan finds it easy to like the children.   5
Sometimes, however, there may be little likable about a child.
"You really have to search for that one tiny, tiny thing that's
good," she says with a smile. The therapist must understand
that the child's undesirable behavior is caused by his or her
inability to cope with internal pain and confusion. The line of
communication must be opened, and some small contact or
mutual understanding must be reached, so that the therapist
can help the patient.

On Tina's second visit, the girl again refused to leave the   6
waiting room until Jan leaned down and whispered in her ear,
"You don't have to throw a tantrum to get to sit on my lap." Tina
looked surprised, then stood up and followed Jan to her office.
"She just wasn't getting enough affection from her parents,"
Jan states simply.

The patient's first three sessions are devoted to evaluation—   7
meeting with the parents and child, determining the cause

of the problem, and making a recommendation for treatment. The therapist may decide to give the case to a co-worker who might be better able to deal with the child's problem. "If you feel you won't be able to get along with the family or child, you don't take the case," Jan explains. "Or if the issue concerns something you're not comfortable with yourself, you don't take the case because it will come out in the session."

Usually, Jan spends half of the hour-long session counsel- 8 ing the child and the other half counseling the parents. The therapy process must involve a close relationship among the child, parents, and therapist. There needs to be a collective effort to resolve the child's problems; everyone must work together. "I've had some parents I just didn't like. I had to give those cases to someone else," Jan admits. Occasionally, she says, parents drop off their child as though "They're getting their car worked on. They come back an hour later and expect their child to be fixed. It just doesn't work that way." However, according to Jan, most parents believe they are responsible for their child's problems. Their willingness to begin therapy signals a desire for improvement and a change for the better.

The remainder of the session Jan spends with the child. 9 Usually, the older the child, the better able he or she is to represent himself for herself as an individual, and the more time will be spent counseling the child alone. "But it's necessary to remember the child is going to have a one-sided view of the situation," Jan cautions. And, in all sessions, the therapist must become someone the child can trust. The relationship is a complicated one. "It's a fine, fine line," she says. "You're their friend, you're not their friend. You're their parent, you're not their parent."

In between sessions, Jan explains, a therapist must try not to 10 worry about the family. She must learn not to "take work home" and realize she can't live the patient's life. "At the end of the day, you do go home. The door does close," Jan says seriously.

Jan's office, located near the back of the building, is one of 11 the larger ones. She chose the furniture herself and tried to create an atmosphere comfortable for all her clients—the teenagers, the adults, and the younger children. The office is paneled and carpeted in brown. On the walls, Jan has hung a few pictures: nature photographs, a drawing of a hand putting flowers in a vase, a garden calendar, and a bright blue embroidered square cloth lighten the dark colors of the room. Next to the door, a white wipe-off chalkboard hangs directly above a small table with orange-and-blue plastic chairs. One small window overlooks the gray concrete of a building five feet away. Her desk has a few papers spread across it. In their midst, a miniature fuzzy blue elephant hangs his trunk over the face of a small electric clock. Holding the rest of Jan's records and paper work is a filing cabinet, buried beneath a mound of assorted psychology books. At the other end of the room are three light-blue cushioned chairs. Two small wicker tables, one with a box of Scotties, sit in between the chairs. Beneath them, covering part of the carpet, are two dust-blue woven rugs. Unnoticeable at first is the lack of knick-knacks and breakable objects.

The clinic lets the individual therapists use their own techniques for therapy. Jan, like most of the other therapists, believes in a dynamic developmental theory that recognizes people all have their own psychological and emotional ends and that not everyone reaches the same stage of development at the same time. Jan sometimes plays a "squiggle game" with her young patients. She and the child sit in front of the chalkboard and pick a colored marker from a box. First, Jan makes a squiggle, and the child makes a picture from it. Then, the child makes a squiggle and Jan draws a picture. The game continues as Jan tries to create a story with the pictures, a story that relates to the child's problem. "I had one child who kept drawing food no matter what kind of squiggle I drew," Jan mentioned. "When I asked him if he'd skipped eating breakfast that morning, he said, 'Naw, I ate some eggs'." Jan finally determined that he wasn't getting enough attention at home. He wasn't abused, he just needed to be cuddled and held more and needed to know his parents cared for him. "Food," she says, "represents the basic idea of nurturing." 12

On average, most children remain in therapy for four to six months. Some cases may last a month; some are longer. Jan's longest case, an abused child named Bryan, lasted seven years. Bryan came with an uncontrollable temper. His emotional 13 problems were complicated when his foster parents began having marital problems. Eventually, the parents divorced and Bryan continued living with the mother. He ended up feeling very close to the mother and feeling he was part of a family. As he grew older, he needed therapy less and less, and finally reached the point where he would call for an appointment only when he knew he was having problems he couldn't solve himself. "When a child stops needing therapy, he begins making comments like, 'I could be out with my friends instead of sitting here talking to you'," Jan laughs, her eyes sparkling. At that point, the therapist feels rejection, as any parent does, yet is happy for the child. It is Jan's job to help the child grow into an individual and live his or her own life — even though she can see all that the child still doesn't know. It is a good feeling, however, to know the child will always remember the therapy as an important part of his or her life.

Jan plans to be a therapist until she retires, maybe starting 14 a private practice some day. "I'm already thirty-eight," she says. "I will probably just take fewer aggressive children when I can't crawl around on the floor or chase them when they throw tantrums." Her energy and vivaciousness show on her face. "I love my work. It's wonderful to see children like Sara, Bryan, and Tina thriving." The room seemed a little brighter as she smiled.

Call Me Eydie May

■   ■   ■

Katy Reising

University of Cincinnati
Cincinnati, Ohio

"Hey, good-looking! Whatcha got cooking?" the old man   1
flirts.

"Not much, old-timer. Did they let you out on good behav-   2
ior?" teases the woman, who is about sixty and still quite attractive.

This spunky lady is Edith Schreiber, known to most of us as   3
Eydie May. She is a cashier at Discount Produce, a small neighborhood market. When asked why she likes working there, she
says, "I love being around people, and I get to see a lot of old
friends who shop here."

I met Eydie May a few years ago when I first went to work   4
at Discount Produce, and never have I met anyone so carefree
and fun. She is so full of humor and wit that she can have fun
doing anything.

She pops open a grocery bag as she begins ringing up the   5
next order, all the while bantering with the customer, a
grandpa who wants to show her photos of his grandkids.

"Those grandbabies are sure good-lookin'. They must take   6
after your wife's side of the family," she laughs, as she counts
out Grandpa's change.

Edith Marie Schreiber was born on May 17, 1927, to Cret-   7
tie and Louis Inabnitt, the youngest of four children. She has

two sisters, Helen and Carol, and one brother, Cecil. "I have many happy memories of my family," she says of her childhood. "I still remember telling spooky stories with my brother and sisters out in our backyard. We had so much fun just making stuff up in our heads. We didn't have many toys then, and there wasn't much to do in Lockland, Ohio, so we had to be creative. But I think that's why we had so much fun together, because between the four of us we made up many different games."

Edith switched schools a lot, but she remembers each name: Peaslee Elementary, Webster Elementary, Arlington Heights, Rothenburg Jr. High, Lockland High, and Woodward High.   8

"I liked going to school. In grade school, I won many awards for spelling, and in high school I loved to play sports. I was on the basketball team and the swimming team," she recalls. "My favorite subject was always arithmetic, but it wasn't my best," reminisces Edith. "Then, when I was fifteen, I started to slack off in school because I got a job at Kahn's Meat Packing Plant. I didn't slack off long though, because as soon as my father saw my grades, I immediately straightened out! Bad grades were one thing my father wouldn't stand for."   9

Edith is wearing her new Guess jeans, and she looks great. Her shirt bears the slogan, "Cows may come, and cows may go, but the bull goes on forever." Her face is golden from the tanning salon next door. Two turquoise plastic combs pull her frosted hair back from her temples. There's a gold chain with a mezuzah around her neck.   10

Fashionable glasses frame Edith's smiling, blue eyes. She wears just a little eyeliner to define her eyes, and a hint of blush to highlight her high cheekbones. On her fingers, Edith sports a few of her favorite rings: one is her diamond wedding ring, and the others are made of sapphires and diamonds. Edith says of her rings, "I appreciate the good things like these in life, because it has taken me a long time to save up for these beauties."   11

There are no customers in line now, so Edith leans against the counter and takes a deep breath. "I'm not really sure why people call me Eydie May," she confides. "It's something my   12 sister Carol used to call me, and it just stuck. But I do wish they would call me Eydie Gorme instead! When I was younger I always pretended to be Eydie Gorme. I would stand in front of the mirror lip-synching her songs on the radio. When my sisters and I put on shows for our parents, imitating our favorite singers or actresses, I was always Miss Eyde Gorme!"

Edith has been married for forty-four years to Harrold 13 Schreiber, a retired brewery worker. "We met at a dance when I was seventeen and he was eighteen," she says. "I loved to jitterbug and he was a good dancer, so we got together. A year later we were married by the Justice of the Peace in Newport, Kentucky. We didn't have much money, so there was no reception or honeymoon, but nonetheless we were happy."

"He has managed to get under my skin after all this time. If 14 you want to know my old man's most annoying habit, you better get out a lot more paper," she chuckles, shaking her head. "The thing that annoys me the most, though, is when he talks to the TV. I try to tell him that he's not gonna get an answer, but he doesn't care as long as there is somethin' to yell at."

Edith loves to joke, but she also has a more serious, sen- 15 timental side. Reflecting on her life, she recalls two especially happy moments in her life. "The first was when I held my oldest daughter, Judy, for the first time after she was born. The second was when I first held Dianna, my youngest daughter. I am very close to my daughters even though Dianna lives in Nebraska, and Judy lives in Illinois. My saddest memory is of Judy's divorce. I couldn't stand to see her hurting like she was, but there was nothing I could do."

Edith has strong opinions about raising children. Love 16 and respect come first, she believes, and continues, "I think parents should teach a child about God, because children who know about God grow up with better values and a strong sense of conscience. I was raised as a Baptist and went to church with my parents every Sunday. I received an award for attending Sunday School every weekend for five years in a row. I think my belief in God has helped me through many difficult times. I also think that raising my daughters in my husband's Catholic faith has helped them to make the right choices."

"Children need to be taught to respect others. I hate to see   17
a child be disrespectful of others, especially of the people who
take care of him. When I was a child, I never dared to talk back
to my parents or any other of my elders. Today it is different
though, because some parents do not exercise enough discipline with their children," she sighs, shaking her head again.

Asked to describe herself, she says, "I guess my best quality   18
is that I don't like to argue with people. The best way to solve
a problem is for people to listen to each other's point of view.
Yelling only makes things worse. Arguing just leads to hasty,
hurtful words that can damage a relationship. That's why I try
very hard to keep away from arguments."

Edith's moods can go from one extreme to another. One   19
minute she's the fun-loving Eydie May, teasing customers, and
the next she's consoling a friend whose husband needs open-
heart surgery. Whether she's making jokes or being a sym-
pathetic listener, however, Edith always shows people that she
cares.

Edith has various talents. She works part-time as a cashier   20
to finance her many hobbies. One of her favorites is photography. She loves taking pictures and organizing them in albums.
Edith also enjoys sewing and knitting such things as scarves,
fancy pieces, and hats. Of all her hobbies, however, Edith says
"Shopping is the one I'm best at. My sister Carol even bought
me one of those 'Shop 'Til You Drop' buttons."

Thanksgiving is her favorite holiday, probably because she   21
gets to see her daughter and grandchildren. She confesses also
that she loves "to eat all of that good food."

"I have a lot to be thankful for," Edith says. "I have a loving   22
family and beautiful grandkids, and lots of friends. That's
what's important, you know. I thank the Lord I still have all my
marbles."

Some customers are waiting in line — it's time to get back to   23
work. Waving to a tall blonde in a jogging suit Edith calls,
"Come on down here to register two." Snapping open a grocery
bag, she starts the next order.

Chapter 5

Reporting Information

The essays in this section were all written by experts. Or rather, they were written *from a position of expertise* attained by the writers through experience, research, or a combination of the two.

A wonderful example of what students can do when they write from their own experience and careful observation, Tamera Helms' essay uses the chronological narrative as a rough framework on which to build a remarkably detailed and interesting account of what goes into a shrimper's day.

In Kent Burbank's essay, there is a more noticeable move back and forth between personal experience and supplementary background material. Here the subject may dictate the method, since allergies and their treatments probably vary far more than shrimping routines. Still, Burbank is close enough to his subject, and familiar enough with it, that he doesn't need to formally document the information he may have gotten from talking to his doctor or reading pamphlets in the waiting room.

Chris Strickland and Ilana Newman do document their sources, and so their papers more closely resemble the traditional research paper. But their individual styles are quite different, and may appeal to different readers. Strickland's essay about bed bugs is informal and humorous, designed to draw us into a subject we had no previous interest in. Newman's essay about the proposed English Language Amendment, more formal and academic in tone, was written as the first part of a two-part "documented argument" assignment. After researching all sides of a controversy, as she did in the paper included here, she went on in a later paper to argue in favor of a particular position.

Lessons in Shrimping

. . .

Tamera Helms

University of North Carolina at Wilmington
Wilmington, North Carolina

"It's stupid to throw fish to those gulls," the captain said for   1
the dozenth time.

"But Daddy they're hungry," I cried.   2

"All right, Sis, but you're gonna regret it."   3

Two fish later I learned what he'd meant when a big white   4
sea gull returned with a fish, like the ones I'd so generously
thrown to him, only in a smellier and more liquid form. This
was one of the many lessons I learned during the summers I
worked on my father's shrimp boat. Shrimping, I was soon to
learn, was much more complicated and interesting than just
pulling up a net full of shrimp.

A shrimper's day starts long before sunrise, usually   5
between 3:30 and 5 AM, depending on how far out the boat's
headed that day. There are even times when a captain will keep
the boat out overnight so as to have first crack at the prior day's
hot spots. In Texas, where I learned about shrimping, the first
"drag" (as pulling the net underwater is called) can't be started
until the sun has fully crossed the horizon, but in the light
before full sunrise the captain or a deckhand puts the net into
the water to be rinsed and soaked. The net ranges in length
from twenty to forty feet on an average sized boat, which is
itself forty to fifty feet long. At this hour many shrimpers use

61

a miniature net to look for the best spot to begin the first drag. This mini net, called a "try net," gives shrimpers some idea of what they'll catch without having to waste much time or fuel.

As soon as the sun is up and the captain has chosen a spot, 6 they "put over the big rig." Having already put the net in the water, they need only to put in the huge wooden "doors" (which resemble the doors on an ancient castle) to spread open the mouth of the net and hold it underwater. It is, however, a size-able task, since the doors may weigh in excess of 150 pounds. A winch is used to lift the doors up off the deck. Then the captain must swing the doors out over the water by revving the engine and causing the boat to jump quickly forward. At that exact moment, he must release the winch brake, dropping the heavy doors into the water. If he fails to get the doors out over the water they could very easily put a hole in the deck or be damaged themselves. Next he must adjust the length of cable let out. If he doesn't let out enough, the net will catch only fish; if he lets out too much, the net may bog down in mud, or, worse, hit an old wreck and maybe destroy the net. Each time shrimpers put the rig over, they are risking two to three thou-sand dollars of equipment.

It would seem that the next hour or two would be just a 7 waiting period, but instead the captain must monitor the cables and depth finder closely. Many shrimpers also monitor their catch with a try net to avoid pulling for shrimp that aren't there. After an hour or two the captain usually picks up the net, although three-hour drags are not uncommon. Using the winch again, he pulls the doors to the top of the water and, using a method similar to the one for dropping the doors, places them back in their rack. Then, using a rope tied to the bag of the net, he pulls the net up beside the boat. Using another rope and the winch again, he lifts the bag of the net up over the deck and unties the end, letting all the contents spill out. At this point the captain decides, from looking at the catch, whether to put it back over or to look for a better place.

Once the first catch of the day is pulled up, the real work 8 starts. "Culling," as most people refer to it, is the art of separat-ing the shrimp from the myriad ocean creatures pulled out of the water. The majority of these creatures are harmless:

croakers, spots, blow fish, baby flounder, trout, and whiting. Others, however, pose dangers to the culler. Crabs, sting rays, eels, jelly fish, hard heads, and sea leeches must be avoided, and thus slow the culler down.

The most dangerous of them is the hard head. Hard heads 9 are saltwater catfish, usually from two inches to a full foot in length, all equally threatening. What makes these fish so dangerous is the poisonous barbs around their head. These very sharp barbs can cut skin badly, shooting a poisonous venom into the cut. This poison causes the wound to swell enormously and painfully. Some people even become sick to their stomach and may run a slight fever. When struck by a hard head, the experienced culler will immediately try to force the wound to bleed and thus push out the poison.

There is, of course, more to culling than just avoiding hard 10 heads. Depending on the ratio of fish to shrimp and the size of the shrimp, there are three different culling procedures. Each begins, however, with the clearing out of the crabs. The pile of shrimp and fish and other creatures is turned over again and again with a shovel to free any crabs that might be lurking underneath. Then the majority of them are pushed out the scupper holes in the side of the railing. Next the deckhand decides whether to cull from the deck of the boat or on a table (which usually doubles as an ice box). If the shrimp are big and easy to see and grab, culling is usually done on the deck by picking up the shrimp and raking the "trash fish" overboard. If the shrimp are small and there are not too many of them, the deckhand shovels loads of the mix onto the table top, picks the fish out of the shrimp, and throws them over the side. He then rakes the remaining shrimp into baskets at his feet. The last method, and the most ingenious, is for a load that has just as many fish as shrimp in it. The deckhand uses an invention called a "salt barrel" to separate the fish from the shrimp. A salt barrel is a tub of seawater with a large amount of extra salt dissolved in it. The excess salt causes the fish to float to the top of the water, where they can be scooped out and thrown back into the bay. Then, using the net, the deckhand dips deep into the barrel and pulls out the remaining shrimp. Any fish that are left are picked out and thrown over. When the culling is finished, the shrimp are iced down and the deck is cleaned of all remaining ocean creatures.

Then, depending on the speed of the deckhand, there may 11 be time to rest a few minutes before the next load is brought up. And so the work continues until sundown, at which time the captain pulls up the last drag of the day and turns the boat toward the port, to sell the day's catch.

At the dock they unload the catch into metal tubs, with 12 holes at the bottom. The shrimp are washed to melt any ice that might add weight to the scales and are then weighed and counted. The "count" indicates the size of the shrimp and is determined by counting the number of shrimp to a pound.

It is at this time that shrimpers find out if they've made any 13 money for the day, or if they've just broken even with the boat's overhead expenses. Despite what people may believe, shrimpers don't make a very prosperous living. It could cause one to wonder why they continue to work under these conditions. Some are trapped into it due to lack of a formal education. They know shrimping, and so that's what they do. Others, such as my father, do it because they love nature. They are addicted to the salt air, the freedom of being on the water, the beautiful sunrises and sunsets. These shrimpers pass their respect and love for nature on to their children. Often this is as simple as warning them to watch for bird bombs. Whatever their reasons for shrimping, they each deserve respect and admiration. The work they do is much harder than most of us will ever know.

The Allergic Nightmare

■   ■   ■

Kent R. Burbank

University of North Dakota
Grand Forks, North Dakota

Millions of people worldwide suffer from daily sneezes 1
and sniffles. The cause of their discomfort—allergies. The
number of substances people can be allergic to is virtually
unlimited. Because most people either have, may develop, or
know someone with allergies, it is important to gain a better
understanding of this affliction.

I am one of the millions plagued with allergies. Coming in 2
contact with something I am allergic to, such as dust and
pollen during fall harvest, causes me terrible physical discomfort. The onset of an allergy attack is always forecast by a tingl-
ing and scratching sensation in my throat. From here, the
torture progresses to my eyes, which burn and itch as though a
thousand pounds of pressure are being applied directly to my
head, quickly producing a terrible headache. Uncontrollable
sneezing and a runny nose follow. Finally, if the attack is severe
or prolonged, I feel as though someone is standing on my
chest, preventing me from breathing.

Although I experience these various symptoms, there are a 3
few symptoms others suffer that I have not encountered, such
as rashes, hives, coughing, swelling, and stomach upset. In
addition, some people have more severe allergic reactions—
extreme breathing difficulty and dangerous drops in blood

pressure, for instance. This type of allergic reaction is referred to as anaphylactic shock and can result in death if the victim is not given immediate medical treatment.

Allergy-sensitive people usually experience anaphylactic 4 shock only when the substance they are allergic to is induced directly into their bloodstream, allowing the substance to spread rapidly throughout their body. For example, I might experience anaphylactic shock if I were stung by a bee, since I am highly allergic to insect bites. Similarly, this reaction might occur if a person sensitive to penicillin were mistakenly injected with it.

Before these noticeable reactions occur in my body, a war 5 is taking place internally. For reasons still not clear, when I come in contact with certain substances known as allergens, harmless visitors to most people, my body mistakes them for enemies. In response, my body sends forth its antibodies to fight what it perceives as invaders. The two sides clash releasing noxious fumes called histamine. The histamine produced by this war is the direct cause of the aggravating symptoms I experience.

No one knows for certain why some people's bodies iden- 6 tify these visitors as harmful while others' do not. I, like many people, inherited some or all of these tendencies. Thus the allergic reaction occurred automatically upon initial exposure to the allergen. For some people, however, this tendency is not inherited. Upon initial exposure, their body simply *learned* to react to a substance, and the symptoms recurred when they were exposed to the same agent again.

All of the symptoms that allergy-sensitive people experi- 7 ence may be initially triggered or worsened by outside factors. These allergy-inducing or heightening factors, such as infection, fatigue, emotional stress, pollution, weather changes, and exercise, explain why some people react to allergens severely one day and then only slightly the next. For example, when I participated in high-school track I often experienced headaches, a runny nose, and breathing difficulties after I had run, even though I felt fine beforehand.

After experiencing many of these symptoms and visiting 8 the doctor several times, I was told that I should be retested for allergies even though I had been tested as a child. The doctor explained to me that this retesting was necessary because as people grow older, they may grow out of certain allergies or may gain new ones. These alterations in allergic sensitivity can occur because of changes within the body as well as in the environment.

The allergy testing was not very difficult or painful. My 9 doctor used the scratch-and-prick test, one of the most commonly used procedures, making several scratches on my arms with needles dipped in different possible allergens. I then waited about thirty minutes for any reaction. Within the waiting period several of the skin pricks changed into red bumps, each a different size and shape. My arms began to burn and itch. When my doctor returned, he measured the bumps and the surrounding redness and recorded the results. From these test results, he determined what substances I was allergic to and roughly how severe the allergies were.

Many allergy-sensitive people must undergo further test- 10 ing because all of their allergies were not revealed by the first test. There are three possible additional tests: laboratory tests, patch tests, and elimination diets. Laboratory tests measure specific levels of certain cells in patients' bodies by testing either their blood or their urine. Patch tests reveal allergies people have to substances that touch their skin. The final test, called an elimination diet, is used by doctors to determine possible food allergies in allergy-sensitive people.

After my doctor determined what I was allergic to, he 11 explained the four main methods of allergy treatment: avoidance, antihistamines, synthetic chemicals, and desensitization. The first treatment he prescribed for me was antihistamines. Antihistamines work by counteracting the histamine produced by the body when the allergens come in contact with the antibodies. The major drawback of antihistamines is that they cause drowsiness and make concentration difficult.

He has also occasionally prescribed for me synthetic corti- 12 sone injections, often known by the brand name Kenalog. These injections are always very effective in providing relief by suppressing the allergy symptoms for several weeks. However, I cannot take the Kenalog shots over an extended period of

Kent R. Burbank

time because the chemical begins to suppress glandular and adrenal functions. These glandular secretions regulate most of the basic bodily functions, including heart rate; therefore, suppressing these secretions is extremely dangerous.

Avoiding the allergy-causing substance is often the easiest 13 and most effective form of treatment if people can actually eliminate the allergen from their environment. For example, the doctor told me to avoid bees as much as possible. However, many people cannot avoid certain allergens because they are constantly exposed to them in their environment. For example, I cannot easily avoid dust and pollen.

I have been undergoing the last method of treatment, 14 desensitization, for approximately a year. The treatment consists of injections of minimal doses of the allergens given at regular intervals in an effort to produce new antibodies to reduce the severity of my reactions. However, there are drawbacks to desensitization. First, it is often extremely difficult to detect everything a person is allergic to and even more difficult to determine the severity of the possible reaction. Therefore, a doctor has difficulty in developing the right serum for each individual. The second major drawback is that desensitization takes a long time before it produces any visible benefit.

Millions of people worldwide regularly suffer from burn- 15 ing eyes, congestion, runny noses, rashes, coughs, breathing difficulties, and many other irritating symptoms. Although these symptoms are often mistaken for colds or other illnesses, the real culprits are allergies. Unfortunately, understanding the complexities of allergies—their causes, symptoms, and treatments—is extremely important.

Bed Bugs

■　■　■

Chris Strickland

Seminole Community College
Sanford, Florida

Are you aware that every night as you snuggle into your
warm and cozy bed, a few tiny friends are squirming in there
right beside you? They have eight long, hairy legs which are
perfectly suited for creeping into tight spots—namely the
covers, your pajamas, or wherever. Their sparsely haired, bean-
shaped bodies are strong and durable enough to withstand the
sudden WHUMPH! of someone jumping onto their snug
domain. Long, antlike mandibles allow them to eat a couple of
delicacies they simple adore: flakes of dead skin or, if they're in
the mood, the dirt under your toenails (Moser 111). These little critters flourish mostly under the top layers of the mattress
(Steier). Lucky for us since we must share our midnight
retreats with up to two million of these adorable little fellows
(Moser 111). You could call them bed bugs, but their proper
name is Dermatophagoides Farinae, the common dust mite
(110). These little guys lead a fascinating life which is simple,
perilous, and sometimes harmful.

A dust mite's existence is by no means extraordinary, but
neither is it trivial. Contrary to popular belief, they play an
important role in our lives by devouring the 50 million or so
skin scales our bodies shed every day (Moser 110). Consequently, you'll find the largest concentrations of them in the

69

bedroom, where people spend one third of their time sleeping and grooming (Steier). They also thrive in carpeting, upholstery, stuffed furniture, and dust balls ("Geographical . . ."; Moser 110). These areas foster countless numbers of mite families. A female mite can produce 25 to 50 eggs which will go through a gestation process of about 6 days before they hatch. Newly born mitelings then pass through a larval and two nymphal stages before they mature. A fully matured male dust mite can expect to survive 60 to 80 days while females live out an impressive 100- to 115-day lifespan (Steier). During that time they'll generally reside in the area of their birthplace, movement having been hampered by their .3 mm size (Norman). As acarologist Edward Baker puts it, "For them to walk from one apartment to another would be like you walking from Washington D.C. to California." Not only does this handicap restrict their ability, but it also subjects them to many household dangers.

The greatest amongst those is the "great wind," better know 3 to us as the common household vacuum cleaner (Moser 111). To dust mites it's nothing less than a full blown 250 mph hurricane. Experience, however, has taught them to utilize this seemingly cataclysmic event to their favor. Whenever the suction whips them up into the air, they simply close up like a turtle and endure the bumpy ride into the vacuum cleaner bag. There they can live by the thousands, happily munching on a fresh supply of dead skin whenever you use the vacuum (qtd. in Moser 111).

Although these little guys are generally harmless, to peo- 4 ple allergic to dust mites they pose a real health problem. Generally, the problem doesn't fall on the mite itself, but the 20 or so feces they excrete every day (111). These clear, marblelike excretions are so light that they float through the air and are constantly being inhaled by us. Unfortunately there is no effective way to minimize their numbers. A study at the University of Southern California found that a bed vacuumed 4 times daily removed only 4.5 percent of the population (Steier). A solution of tannic acid applied regularly to problem areas helps minimize the allergen as will covering mattresses and

pillowcases with plastic zipper cases ("Dust"). Tolerance, however, is probably the only viable solution.

Now before you decide to sleep in the bathtub or on the   5
kitchen floor tonight, try to look at dust mites this way.
Without them we'd be up to our necks in dust and literally
swimming in dead skin. Think of them as tiny household ser-
vants who work tirelessly at making your job of cleaning house
somewhat easier. With that in mind, hit your pillow a little
softer tonight, flap those covers a little less, and remember to
wish your newfound friends a good night. Who knows, you
may wake up in the morning with great-looking toenails.

Works Cited

Allergic Rhinitus. Videocassette. Dir. Hollester Steier. Pharmacin,
   1987.
"Dust Mites: What Are They Anyway?" *Update: Semoran Allergy Clinic
   Newsletter*. Casselberry, FL.: Semoran Allergy Clinic, 1989.
Porth, Eli. *Geographical and Environmental Factors in the Distribution of
   Dermaphagoides Mites*. Casselberry, FL.: Semoran Allergy Clinic.
Moser, Penny Ward. "All the Real Dirt on Dust." *Discover*, Nov. 1986:
   106–115.
Norman, Phillip S. *Antigens That Cause Atopic Disease*. Vol. 2 of *Immunio-
   logical Diseases*. 2 vols. Boston: Little, Brown, 1965:780–781.
"Tannic Acid Makes Mites Bite the Dust." *Prevention*, Dec. 1984:8.

The Proposed English
Language Amendment

■   ■   ■

Ilana Newman

University of Arizona
Tucson, Arizona

The drive for a common language in the United States is   1
far from a new issue. Language is not mentioned in the Constitution, yet many believe that English's "predominant status
among the Framers . . ." (Lexion 658) is suggested by the fact
that the document was written in English. Others contend that
the subject of language was deliberately omitted in order to
attract immigrants to the new country. In the early twentieth
century, the question of a national language arose once again
as a new surge of immigrants to the United States posed a
threat to the status quo with their different languages and cul-
tures. This movement, known as Americanization, gained support and its proponents believed that "any continuing cultural
and linguistic ties to Old World countries would create a
chasm between the immigrants and established Americans"
(Lexion 660). The roots of this fear were reflected in the passage of the Naturalization Act of 1906, which required immigrants applying for citizenship to be able to sign their names
and speak English "to the satisfaction of a naturalization examiner" (Leibowicz 533). World War I also brought about hostility

to Germans and other foreigners. As a result, fifteen states passed laws making English the only language of instruction in primary schools.

Legislation for an English Language Amendment (ELA) to   2
the Constitution appeared in 1981 and 1983, and in 1985 two different versions were introduced. The Senate version read: "Section 1. The English language shall be the official language of the United States. Section 2. The Congress shall have the power to enforce this article by appropriate legislation" (Lexion 662). In contrast, the House version proposed:

> *Section 1.* The English language shall be the official language of the United States.
>
> *Section 2.* Neither the United States nor any State shall require by law, ordinance, regulation, order, decree, program, or policy, the use in the United States of any language other than English.
>
> *Section 3.* This article shall not prohibit any law, ordinance, regulation, order, decree, program, or policy requiring educational instruction in a language other than English for the purpose of making students who use a language other than English proficient in English.
>
> *Section 4.* The Congress and the States may enforce this article by appropriate legislation (Lexion 662–663).

Will passage of such amendments lead to the greater unity of the citizens of the Unites States, or is this too severe a solution to a problem that can be solved otherwise?

The forecast claim of proponents of the ELA is that English   3
is the common bond between all people in the United States and, unless precautions are made to protect it, we will no longer be a "united" nation. This idea is reflected in John Jay's criteria for nationhood:

> A large expanse of connected, continuous territory
>
> A common language
>
> Attachment to the same principles of government
>
> Similarity of manners and customs

A long and common history of war, suffering, and a happy outcome

Readiness to forget past intergroup conflicts (Leibowicz 527).

Of these, only two still apply to the present-day United States: a common language and a commitment to democracy—and the latter is sometimes questioned. A popular example of what our future may hold is found in Canada, where a single form of government is not enough to overcome the separation caused by its two languages. Unless the bond of English is strengthened, ELA supporters say, our future might lie along the same lines. English is spoken in more than forty countries, it is one of the two languages used by the United Nations (French is the other), and it is the language in which two thirds of all scientific papers are published ("The New English Empire" 127). By not affirming our status as an English-speaking country, we are acting in the opposite direction of the current worldwide trend.

The ELA's critics, however, recognize the importance of   4
English as a strong connection, but insist it is not the only existing one. They cite Switzerland as a prime example of four languages peacefully coexisting within the same country. Instead, they claim, democracy, freedom, and equal opportunities are integral provisions of our Constitution and, therefore, pertain to all of us. Immigrants come to this country to enjoy rights they are refused elsewhere, not so they can communicate with other Americans. Because of this fact, opponents of the ELA believe it is the democratic bond alone that has kept our country together, even with the diversity of languages spoken here. They stress that the validity of the English language itself is not in question, but rather the side effects of making it the official language.

While the importance of English as a link between those   5
who have little else in common is clear, the true controversy lies in other issues. One of the most heated debates deals with printing election ballots only in English, instead of in two or (in the case of San Francisco) three languages. One of the fundamental constitutional rights granted to all citizens is

the right to vote. In *Reynolds* v. *Sims* (1964) the Supreme Court
rules:

> [T]he right of suffrage is a fundamental matter in a free and
> democratic society. Especially since the right to exercise the
> franchise in a free and unimpaired manner is a preservative
> of other basic civil and political rights, any alleged infringe-
> ment of the right of citizens to vote must be carefully and
> meticulously scrutinized (Lexion 673).

Opponents of the ELA feel that passing the amendment   6
would be tantamount to imposing an English proficiency
requirement on any foreign-speaking minority otherwise entitled to vote. Of course, such voters would not be refused entry
into voting booths; but if they couldn't read the ballots, they
would be at a distinct disadvantage — in essence, disenfran-
chised.

ELA advocates maintain that learning English is necessary   7
for a person to fully function in American society. They sug-
gest that English-only ballots would heighten the incentive for
immigrants to learn English and become "more American."
Still, many will vote without exposure to the candidates or
propositions of an election, but this is not uncommon practice now. Many English-speaking citizens don't take time to
consider the issues they are voting on; yet they go to the polls
every election because it is their duty as "good Americans."
Already, the federal and county governments have started to
reduce the number of places where ballots are required —
usually where less than ten percent of the population needs
them ("¡Caramba!" 33).

The foregoing discussion reveals that the arguments sur-   8
rounding an all-English ballot have constitutional ramifica-
tions. Only a court can determine whether or not the ELA is
unconstitutional. However, the views on whether or not bilingual studies are helpful in learning English are based mainly
on opinion.

According to ELA adversaries, bilingual education is very   9
important in making the transition from speaking a minority
language to speaking English. These programs allow immi-

grants to function in society while they are learning, so they do not have to wait until they have mastered English before they can exercise their rights. In addition, studies show that today's immigrants learn English at the same rate, or faster, than immigrants one hundred years ago — proof that bilingual services do not hinder the speed with which one learns English (Lexion 679).

Champions of the ELA, however, believe that bilingual services serve only as a crutch that immigrants can fall back on when their English proves insufficient. Knowing that they don't have to understand English to get the information they want or need is an excuse to put off an English education indefinitely. Newcomers who are motivated to succeed in American society will learn English readily. Those who are less eager and able to assimilate learn English at a slower pace, and they are the ones who end up dependent on bilingual services (Conklin and Lourie 236). 10

The justifications for and against bilingualism seem to end in a stalemate. What action can be taken today to eliminate the need for these special resources in the future? Opinion differs on whether naturalization requirements should be used to ensure that all the United States citizens can speak English. 11

Those who oppose the ELA feel that the amendment is not the least drastic measure possible to protect the primacy of the English language in the United States. Because Congress regulates naturalization, an alternative would be adding a higher level of English literacy requirement for naturalization (Lexion 680). Eventually, they believe, the need for bilingual services and ballots would therefore disappear. 12

The ELA defenders strongly disagree, pointing out that not all non-English speakers become citizens by naturalization. Puerto Ricans are automatically citizens of the United States by statute, and therefore do not have to satisfy any English language requirement (Lexion 668). The ELA would be the only means to successfully impose the language requirement, they claim. Otherwise, the constant flux of immigrants from Puerto Rico would make the ELA impossible to enforce. 13

Every one of us, whether we agree or disagree strongly   14
about the ELA, can appreciate the movement to protect the
English language. Likewise, all can see that the ELA, in either of
its most current forms, is not perfect. Careful consideration
will ensure that we will not hastily pass an amendment that we
will later regret. Although this may not seem likely at this time,
the past has shown that our government eventually does what
is right.

Works Cited

"¡Caramba!" *Economist* 301 (6 Dec. 1986):33–34.

Conklin, Nancy Faires, and Margaret A. Lourie. *A Host of Tongues.* New York: Free Press, 1983.

Leibowicz, Joseph. "The Proposed English Language Amendment: Shield or Sword?" *Yale Law and Policy Review 3* (Spring 1985):519–550.

Lexion, Valerie. "Language Minority Voting Rights and the English Language Amendment." *Hastings Constitution Law Quarterly 14* (Spring 1987):657–681.

"The New English Empire." *Economist* 301 (20 Dec. 2986):127–131.

▪ Chapter 6 ▪

Taking a Position

How one supports a position on a controversial subject depends on what that subject is and how both writer and reader relate to it.

In the first essay in this chapter, Michael Kingston writes on the legality of eating animals traditionally kept as pets, an issue that is not only unfamiliar to most readers but emotionally charged as well. Wisely, he first provides us with enough information to understand the issue, then gently urges us to think beyond any initial ethnocentric responses we might have.

Julie McDonald's subject—sorority rush—may be more familiar to readers, especially college students and teachers, but it is no less challenging. In fact, it may even be more challenging because of reader biases. McDonald's solution is to introduce the controversy with a lively narrative anecdote, then to use quotes from sorority members to support her argument that the rush system needs to be changed.

Margaret Solomon's topic—capital punishment—is also familiar to readers, which gives her the same challenge McDonald faces. And like McDonald, Solomon chooses to approach her topic from "a personal viewpoint." Some readers may be uncomfortable with Solomon's choice here, preferring a more traditional "objective" stance. But given the history of the capital punishment controversy, and the failure of all "objective" arguments to resolve the question so far, an approach which frankly acknowledges its grounding in personal belief can be refreshing. (It's worth noting, of course, that Solomon buttresses her argument with such traditional forms of support as facts, statistics, and authority, and that she uses formal documentation to enhance her rhetorical appeal.)

Documentation serves an important rhetorical purpose in Connie Russell's essay as well. Because she is taking what may be an unpopular stand on the well-publicized issue of National Park forest fire policy, Russell has the burden of convincing her audience that she knows what she's talking about. This she does very well, by tracing the history and rationale for the "let it burn" policy and showing how opposing views may be based on misconceptions or misinformation.

Especially evident in the last two essays are the writers' efforts to acknowledge and deal with opposing arguments. It might be worth studying the lack of a clear "refutation" section in the first two essays. Is it a significant gap, or is consideration of opposing views simply less necessary there?

Creating a Criminal

■　■　■

Michael Kingston

University of California at Riverside
Riverside, California

In reaction to the Vietnamese-American practice of rais-　1
ing canines for food, Section 598b of the California Penal
Code was recently amended to read as follows:

> (a) Every person is guilty of a misdemeanor who possesses,
> imports into this state, sells, buys, gives away, or accepts any
> carcass or part of any carcass of any animal traditionally or
> commonly kept as a pet or companion with the sole intent of
> using or having another person use any part of that carcass
> for food.
>
> (b) Every person is guilty of a misdemeanor who possesses,
> imports into this state, sells, buys, gives away, or accepts any
> animal traditionally or commonly kept as a pet or compan-
> ion with the sole intent of killing or having another person
> kill that animal for the purpose of using or having another
> person use any part of the animal for food.

This is a fascinating new law, one that brings up a complex　2
set of moral, political, and social questions. For example: What
constitutes a "pet"? Do pets have special "rights" that other
animals aren't entitled to? How should these "rights" be balanced with the real political rights of the human populace?

81

How do we define the civil rights of an ethnic minority whose actions reflect cultural values that are at odds with those of the majority? Section 598b does not mention these issues. Rather, it seems to simply walk around them, leaving us to figure out for ourselves whose interests (if any) are being served by this strange new law.

The first thing one might wonder is whether the purpose 3 of Section 598b is to improve the lot of pets throughout California. What we do know is that it seeks to prevent people from eating animals traditionally regarded as pets (dogs and cats). But for the most part, the only people who eat dogs or cats are Vietnamese-Americans. Furthermore, they don't consider these animals "pets" at all. So, pets aren't really being protected. Maybe section 598b means to say (in a roundabout manner) that *all* dogs and cats are special and therefore deserve protection. Yet, it doesn't protect them from being "put to sleep" in government facilities by owners who are no longer willing to have them. Nor does it protect them from being subjected to painful, lethal experiments designed to make cosmetics safe for human use. Nor does it protect them from unscrupulous veterinarians who sometimes keep one or two on hand to supply blood for anemic pets of paying customers. No, the new law simply prevents Vietnamese-Americans from using them as food.

Is the consumption of dogs or cats so horrible that it 4 merits its own law? One possible answer is that these practices pose a special threat to the trust that the pet-trading network relies upon. Or in other words: that strange man who buys one or more of *your* puppies just might be one of those dog-eaters. But this scenario just doesn't square with reality. A Vietnamese-American, canine-eating family is no more a threat to the pet-trading industry than is a family of European heritage that chooses to raise rabbits (another popular pet) for its food. Predictably, there is a loophole in Section 598b that allows for the continued eating of pet rabbits. Its circular logic exempts from the new law any animal that is part of an *established* agricultural industry.

It seems as though Vietnamese-Americans are the only 5 ones who can't eat what they want, and so it is hard not to think of the issue in terms of racial discrimination. And why shouldn't we? After all, the Vietnamese community in California has long been subjected to bigotry. Isn't it conceivable that latent xenophobia and racism have found their way into the issue of dog-eating? One needs only to look at the law itself for the answer. This law protects animals "traditionally . . . kept as a pet." *Whose* traditions? Certainly not the Vietnamese's.

Of course, the typical defense for racially discriminatory laws such as this one is that they actually protect minorities by forcing assimilation. The reasoning here is that everything will run much smoother if we can all just manage to fall in step with the dominant culture. This argument has big problems. First, it is morally bankrupt. How does robbing a culture of its uniqueness constitute a protection? Second, it doesn't defuse racial tensions at all. Racists will always find reasons for hating the Vietnamese. Finally, any policy that seeks to label minorities as the cause of the violence leveled against them is inherently racist itself. 6

Whatever the motives behind Section 598b, the consequences of the new law are all too clear. The government, not content with policing personal sexual behavior, has taken a large step toward dictating what a person can or cannot eat. This is no small infringement. I may never have the desire to eat a dog, but I'm rankled that the choice is no longer mine, and that the choice was made in a climate of racial intolerance. Whatever happened to the right to life, liberty, and the pursuit of happiness? 7

Unfortunately, we may suffer more than just a reduction in personal choice. Crimes such as dog-eating require a certain amount of vigilance to detect. More than likely, the police will rely upon such dubious measures as sifting through garbage left at curbside, or soliciting anonymous tips. Laws that regulate private behavior, after all, carry with them a reduction in privacy. 8

We sure are giving up a lot for this new law. It's sad that we receive only more criminals in return. 9

Sorority Rush: Just Desserts

■   ■   ■

Julie McDonald

Bowling Green State University
Bowling Green, Ohio

Chewing her fingernails, a tall, blonde woman sits among   1
twenty other nervous members of a sorority rush group. Any
minute the group's Rho Chis (leaders) will walk through the
lobby doors and present each one with her sorority bid. The
tall blonde adjusts the collar of her new "Chaus" sports jacket,
feeling confident that her outfit is perfect for the morning
events. Finally the two smiling Rho Chis appear and pass out
bids. Excited women with trembling hands rip open their final
invitations and run off to greet their new sorority sisters. Happily the woman heads off to the Alpha Zee Delta house, thinking to herself, "Thank God rush week is over and I've been
accepted." Oblivious to her surroundings, she brushes past an
unlucky member of the same rush group. The unfortunate
woman received no bid, only a polite note stating that no
sorority wanted her membership. No one remained in the
room to answer the crying woman as she pleaded, "Why not
me?" Unfortunately for young women who desire a membership in a Bowling Green sorority, the formal rush process
encourages less-than-fair measures in selection.

At Bowling Green rush consists of a set of four social par-   2
ties held throughout the week before Fall semester begins.

Based on her showing at the four parties, each woman will be either accepted or rejected by the sorority of her choice.

Party number one, Open House, requires every rushee to visit all fourteen sororities. Each visit consists of one twenty-minute conversation with one member of the house. Based on the twenty-minute conversations, the sororities decide whether or not they want to invite the rushee back to their next round of parties. The following morning each rushee gets a computer printout listing the houses that have extended invitations to return. No one can return to a house unless she's received an invitation. With their narrowed-down lists of sororities in hand, the rushees head off for party number two.

The following three parties operate on the same format except the amount of time socializing at each house increases and the number of houses visited decreases. By the time a rushee reaches her fourth and final party, Formal Desserts, she has been narrowed down to two sororities for membership. At the completion of all four parties, sororities either extend bids (invitations) for membership or regrets (polite statements of rejection). For the women who receive bids, sorority life begins. For those who receive regrets, rush is over at least until next year.

According to members and supporters of the Greek system, formal rush is the most effective way for young women to find a sorority suited for them. "As a woman goes to each house she gets a feel for the sorority's character," said sophomore Phi Mu member Kristen Ankney. "She will find that she just does not fit in some chapters. The important thing to do is to find a house that shares your character."

Problems arise because of the amount of time given for getting to know the different houses. The entire orientation process allows for a mere three hours of interaction between rushees and sorority members, hardly enough time to get to know one another's "character." "I went through rush and pledged Alpha Chi Omega my freshman year," said senior Susan Guild. "During rush the girls went out of their way to be friendly, but when rush ended so did their friendliness. It bothered me that they were not who I thought they were. Need-

85

less to say, I dropped out of the sorority for that very reason my sophomore year."

Time limitation is not the only factor that can lead to false 7 impressions of a sorority's character. Many houses pair up one rushee with one member during each party, and if, by chance, two people with clashing personalities are paired up, they are likely to part with negative feelings toward each other. The rushee projects her feelings about the one member onto the entire chapter only because she has no one else to base her opinion on. Likewise, the member reports a negative encounter to her sisters and no one can stand up for the rushee because no one else met her. Such methods of evaluation are unfair to both the sororities and the rushees.

The selection of future members is said to be based essen- 8 tially on a rushee's character. Character, the complex mental and ethical traits marking and individualizing a person, is stressed again and again throughout rush. Nevertheless, a hypocritical contradiction occurs at every house through the enforcement of a rush dress code. As each party escalates in importance so does the formality of dress. By the time they reach Formal Desserts, the rushees find themselves wearing costly evening gowns, dining off expensive china—and discussing the character of the sorority they're about to join. Ironically, no one mentions that character is a trait within a person's soul, not in black velvet evening gowns and pearl necklaces.

And some women never make it as far as the second, third 9 or fourth parties. After Open House any woman can receive regrets from all fourteen sororities. Women who receive regrets do not get a refund of their $25 rush fee, nor do they get an explanation. They simply have the option to try again next year, and to hope they can grow into some sorority's "character."

A woman who is considering rushing a sorority at Bowling 10 Green needs to understand the system and to realize the biased methods used in choosing sorority members. In the future, Bowling Green needs to revamp formal rush and, therefore, to make it possible for people of any character to join a sorority.

Capital Punishment: A Personal Viewpoint

• • •

Margaret Solomon

Wright State University
Dayton, Ohio

According to crime statistics in the mid-1980s, more than 1
2.3 million men and over 300,000 women were in state and
federal prisons. These statistics bring the realism of crime very
close to home; and with the thought of crime comes punishment and the ever-controversial question of capital punishment. I, for one, do not acknowledge capital punishment as a
viable form of criminal punishment. I do not blindly accept
that it is an effective crime deterrent; nor do I accept that our
justice system is fit to pass such judgments. I believe that life
imprisonment should be the furthest extent to which a sentence can be carried.

The taking of one human being's life among the myriad 2
criminals presently within the penal system is not going to
cause crime to cease to exist. So few death sentences are actually carried out that the threat of the death penalty has actually
lessened. At most, criminals are more afraid of going to jail for
a long period of time because the death penalty is handed out
so sparingly. At the very least, the judicial system has created
opportunities for criminals to seek stays of execution, which
can prolong their life anyway. Because so few executions are

carried out, they do not help citizens economically. I agree that it costs more money to incarcerate someone and keep them alive than to execute them and that jail overcrowding is a large problem in this country. In fact, the United States prison population has more than doubled in recent decades, from 196,183 in the early 1970s to 503,601 in 1985 (Gottfredson 205). However, I simply do not see how taking away the lives of less than one percent of them is going to save enough money or space to justify a killing. These figures also serve to prove that capital punishment does not deter crime. Now our jails are filled with more prisoners than ever. According to Gottfredson and McConville, authors of *America's Correctional Crisis*, the crime rates hit a peak in 1980 and have been climbing since (161). For capital punishment (or any punishment, for that matter) to be considered effective, crime rates would have to be dropping.

I also do not have enough faith in our elected officials or   3
judicial system to believe they should ever have the authority to end someone's life. Judges and court officials have always been swayed by public opinion and outside forces. In *Fatal Error*, Joseph Shorlitt describes the 1953 Rosenberg espionage trial and executions, stating that a Supreme Court judge blatantly disregarded the Atomic Energy Act of 1946 in order to carry out more expediently a death sentence, what the McCarthy-era public craved (2). I do understand that when we elect officials we are giving up some of our rights to choose by putting the power into their hands. However, I believe if there is a possibility in the slightest that doubt exists, then something as final as death cannot be involved.

I believe, despite the cost, that life imprisonment should   4
be the most severe form of punishment. I agree with Duff when he states, "The strongest reason for a penalty is that it inflicts suffering upon the punishable person . . ." (20). Imprisoned criminals suffer every day they spend incarcerated. In his book *Straight Talk from Prison*, Lou Torok, a lifer presently incarcerated in Ohio's Chillicothe Correctional Institute, describes "what it is like to lose freedom, dignity, and human rights" (29). According to Torok, a convict must live a life without freedom of movement, privacy, or genuine companion-

ship. In prison he or she is subject to severe rules, physical abuse, and great psychological suffering. In fact, from this viewpoint, capital punishment seems to be an easy way out for the inmate. At least death would be easier than living in torment the rest of their lives. Perhaps this reality is why the suicide rate in prisons is so high, and why persons being prepared for execution seem to accept it at the end.

The guilty should be punished, but perhaps our society 5 suffers from what John Conrad calls "inertia abetted by tradition" (1). We are all moving through this world so quickly that it seems we may fail to keep up with the times. Perhaps capital punishment is simply "easy" because we have such a long history with it. But a new decade is upon us, and soon a new century. I believe it's time to find a better way.

Works Cited

Conrad, John P. *Crime and Its Correction*. Berkeley and Los Angeles: University of California, 1965.

Gottfredson, Stephen G. and Sean McConville. *America's Correctional Crisis*. Westport (CT): Greenwood, 1987.

Shorlitt, Joseph H. *Fatal Error*. New York: Scribner's, 1989.

Torok, Lou. *Straight Talk from Prison*. New York: Human Sciences, 1974.

Let It Burn for the Next Generation

■   ■   ■

Connie Russell

University of Arizona

Tucson, Arizona

From June to October 1988, Yellowstone National Park   1
was the site of forty-nine fires, affecting about 1.1 million of its
2.2 million acres. Eight of these fires were caused by humans
and fought as soon as they were noticed. The other forty-one
fires were caused by lightning, which is considered a "natural"
cause of fire (Bagwell B13). Other causes of "natural" fires are
volcanic eruptions and spontaneous combustion. Because the
fires in Yellowstone were classified as "natural," they were allowed to burn under a sixteen-year-old National Park policy—
the "let-it-burn" policy. This policy allows all natural fires to
burn until they burn out or present a danger to life or property. In July, it was obvious that the fires weren't going to put
themselves out and that they posed a threat to the Yellowstone
Inn. As a result, the Interior Secretary, Donald Hodel, started
an effort to put out the fires and any following ones. The
fires were finally extinguished by the end of November 1988.
However, the question remains of whether the "let-it-burn"
policy is the best fire policy for our National Parks and our
environment.

In 1872, the Yellowstone Act set aside Yellowstone as a park   2
"for the benefit and enjoyment of the people in which the
natural curiosities or wonders were to be maintained in their
natural condition" (Graber 19). Even though fires played an
important role in the "natural condition" of the parks before
man set foot on North America, the parks' policy toward fire
was to suppress all fires regardless of how they started. For over
one hundred years, the National Park Service went by this
suppression policy. This caused large amounts of unnatural
build-up such as decaying wood, dead grasses, and debris. This
policy of suppression caused the build-up, which is responsible for the damage caused by the Yellowstone fires, not the
let-it-burn policy which has been the recipient of the blame.
Therefore, the let-it-burn policy should continue. It is more
beneficial to the environment, allowing nature to take care of
itself as it has done for years.

It may help to understand why the National Parks Service   3
changed their fire policy. The change was brought about
because of extensive research done by an advisory board on
wildlife management called the Leopoid Committee. This
board studied the wildlife and vegetation of many national
parks and determined that the years of suppressing fires had
been more harmful than beneficial to the environment. In
order to correct the mistakes made in the past, they suggested
using "controlled fires" to lower the amount of built-up fuel,
then allowing fires caused by lightning to burn without inter-
ference until they "either burned themselves out or threatened
human life, buildings or private property" (Haggerty 28).
These suggestions made up the 1963 Leopoid Report. It wasn't
until 1972 that the National Parks Service changed from a suppression policy to the let-it-burn policy.

Some feel that instead of having the suppression policy or   4
the let-it-burn policy, we should have a modified let-it-burn
policy. They agree that fires are beneficial to the environment
but feel that the fires should be suppressed before they
threaten life or property. The result of this modification would
create a policy which would be impractical to carry out since
fires tend to be complex and unpredictable. The only way the

91

National Parks Service could suppress the fires before any danger to life or property arises is by suppressing them at their onset. This leads back to complete suppression and the build-up of debris that is so dangerous for our environment.

The suppression policy causes damage to the environment 5 by allowing a build-up of debris from dead or dying trees, pine needles, leaves, and garbage brought in by visitors. This makes excellent fuel for a fire, which can be set off by a small spark. Due to the amount of fuel, the result could end up in a fire which burns intensely enough to sterilize the ground. This can make it hard for an area to regenerate, since the seeds and organic matter would have to be brought from other areas.

Even though lots of build-up was left from the suppression 6 policy, sterilization wasn't a major case in Yellowstone. According to Jim Brown, Forest Service researcher of fire effects, the heat of the fire has to penetrate "the soil to a depth of about eighteen inches" in order to pose a threat to regeneration. "And very few acres were burned that deep, maybe only about one percent of the park" (Faybee 45). As for the areas which were burned less severely, they started regeneration about three weeks after the fire had left the area (Milstein 50).

Built-up debris also creates "ecological [deserts]" which 7 contain "little wildlife or plant diversity" (Cutler E31). Before the fires, Yellowstone consisted mainly of 250–400-year-old Lodgepole pines. These trees, like ponderosa pines and Douglas firs, grow very tall and prevent sunlight from reaching the floor of the forest. Between the lack of sunlight and the debris, few seeds make it through germination to become seedlings. Without these seedlings, the herbivores (plant-eating animals) leave, and when they do, so do the carnivores (meat-eating animals) (Faybee 46). This leads to a very uninteresting park, with little or no variation in plant life and only a small variety of wildlife.

After a fire, an environment which contains great diversity 8 in plants and animals evolves. John Varley, Yellowstone's chief scientist, said, "[Fires are a] part of the rebirth and renewal of the park's ecosystem. They represent the end of one life cycle and ensure the beginning of the next" (Lerner 36). This is because fires clear out the undergrowth, claim the least healthy of the plants and animals, and accelerate the return of nutrients to the soil. By ridding the forest of the older, least healthy trees, more sunlight reaches the forest floors. This sunlight, along with new nutrients in the soil, promotes the growth of seedlings. These plants in turn will attract new animals and allow other animals to flourish in the regenerating area. One example of this is the birds in Yellowstone. Ecologists estimate that twelve birds will leave freshly burnt areas because they require the "old growth forests" to live. They also expect eighteen new birds to come to this same area (Rudner 15). This is an increase of six birds. Two of them happen to be rare species: the mountain bluebirds and the three-toed woodpeckers (Milstein 50).

Forest fires also insure the survival of the "fire species" plants. "Fire species" plants are those which can withstand fire and actually need fires to survive and reproduce. One of the most common fire species is the ponderosa pine, which covers over thirty-six million acres of the western United States. The ponderosa pine, like the lodgepole pine of Yellowstone, has needles containing a highly flammable substance called resin. Since the needles dry very quickly, require a long time to decay, and lie on the forest floor in a way which allows air circulation, they are naturally prone to fire. This resin also seals the openings to the cones in which the seeds are kept. Without a fire to open these seals, the cones stay sealed for over twenty years, preventing the pine from reproducing (Poynter 106). 9

Unfortunately, these results of the fires are often not seen until after the fire is extinguished, smoke has settled, and regeneration has begun. Rupert Cutler, former Secretary of Agriculture, feels that "living day after day in stinking, irritating smoke would cause even the most devout environmentalist to question the wisdom of letting fires burn" (Cutler E31). If everyone would wait until the fire was out, they wouldn't be as quick to criticize or place blame as Wyoming's Senators Alan Simpson and Malcolm Wallop were when they requested the resignation of the national Parks Service Director William Penn Mott, Jr. For these reasons, Cutler says that there ought to be a law that no one can make "pronouncements about national park fire policy until the season's last fire is out, when 10 personal discomfort, fear and panic also have been extinguished" (Cutler E31).

To make matters worse for the let-it-burn policy, while the 11
fires were still burning in Yellowstone, the media reports from
Yellowstone implied that half of Yellowstone was being burned
to ashes. This common belief lead to severe criticism of the
let-it-burn policy by the public. Actually, the 1.1 million acre
figure given out by the media was the number of acres "within
fire perimeters." As of mid-October 1988, the National Park
service estimated that within these fire perimeters

> about four hundred forty thousand acres had experienced
> "some burning" and about two hundred twenty thousand
> acres "experienced canopy fires only." About twenty-two
> thousand acres were scorched all to hell. As well, as much as
> five hundred thousand more acres in the national forest
> bordering Yellowstone experienced "some degree of burn-
> ing." (Faybee 42)

It can be seen from these statistics that the fire in Yellowstone
burned at different intensities and levels at different places.
This randomness of fires creates a mosaic containing different
types of vegetation. With areas of forest in different stages of
development, the diversity of animals is greater, since different animals prefer different types of forests.

Unlike *Bambi*, animals don't necessarily get killed in forest 12
fires. This movie led many to believe its implication that a lot
of animals are killed in fires because they can't run away fast
enough to escape them. It is true that some animals do get
killed. In Yellowstone, four buffalo, some small animals such as
squirrels, and insects were killed (Faybee 47). However, these
are normally the older and least healthy wildlife whose elimination is normally better for the rest of the population. "Most
of the smaller animals are burrowers who simply go under-
ground until the fire passes" (Rudner 15). The larger animals
just behave on instinct and walk out of the fire's way. Elk have
even been know to "[bed] down a hundred yards or so from the
flames" (Rudner 15). After regeneration starts, these animals
will return to the area, where there is new food and fewer bugs

to bother them. One exception in Yellowstone may be the grizzlies, who will probably have to leave the park to find enough food for hibernation. According to biologist Tim Clark, this is unfortunate for the grizzlies because "[it] will increase the incidents of contact between bears and man [and] the bears usually lose those" (Faybee 45).

National Parks were set aside to be left "unimpaired for the   13 enjoyment of future generations" (Graber 19). The fires of 1988 have created a new Yellowstone and a controversy over the let-it-burn policy. This policy enables the "natural" conditions of the park to remain as they would have had humans never tampered there. Without the policy, the parks would be impaired, and the purpose of the National Parks would have to be changed. Since Yellowstone was our first National Park, it has always been the leader in major park policy decisions. Hopefully when it comes down to the final decision the let-it-burn policy will be accepted for the benefit of the environment, the wildlife, and the future generations. As Howie Wolke, Yellowstone backcountry guide, said:

> Even if some of the direct effects of fire are sad, it doesn't change the fact that, without past fires, Yellowstone wouldn't have become what it was before these fires. People say they [liked] Yellowstone the way it was? Well, fine. I think we owe it to future generations to make sure Yellowstone regenerates. (Faybee 45).

This regeneration cannot happen without fires and the let-it-burn policy which allows them.

Works Cited

Bagwell, Keith. "Yellowstone Blazes Rejuvenated. . . ." *Arizona Daily Star* 20 Nov. 1988:B13.

Cutler, M. Rupert. "Fire in Yellowstone, Hot Air in D.C." *New York Times* 11 Sept. 1988:E31.

Faybee, M. John. "Yellowstone: Was the Fire a. . . ." *Backpacker* 17 (Jan. 1989):42–47.

Graber, David M. "The Evolution of National Park. . . ." *Fire Management Notes* 46 (?):19–25.

Haggerty, Joe. "Flames of Controversy." *New Scientist* 119 (25 Aug. 1988):28–29.

Lerner, Micheal A. "Yellowstone: Up in Smoke." *Newsweek* (5 Sept. 1988):36.

Milstein, Michael. "The Long, Hot Summer." *National Parks* 62 (Nov.–Dec. 1988):26–27, 50.

Poynter, Margaret. *Wildland Fire Fighting.* New York: Atheneum, 1982.

Rudner, Ruth. "Even as It Burns, Yellowstone Is Reborn." *Wall Street Journal* 25 Aug. 1988:15.

Chapter 7

Proposing Solutions

The essays in this section show what writers can do when they know their subjects well. Three of the essays — "Wheelchair Hell," "WSU Dining Facilities," and "Handling the Pressure" — focus on campus problems that the writers have first-hand knowledge of. The fourth, "Iowa's Dirty Problem" is broader in scope, but still "close to home" for the writer.

In some cases, persuading the reader that there *is* a problem is the writer's primary task. Shannon Long must get non-handicapped readers to see that the partial measures that have so far been adopted at her university simply do not solve the problem of access for the disabled. As a disabled student herself, she is able to use personal experience to make her point quite effectively.

In a similar manner, Chad Friesen uses both anecdotal evidence and quotes from other students to support his argument that university students face serious stress problems. Because his proposed solutions extend and modify structures that already exist on campus, they are likely to strike his audience as worthwhile and practical.

The audience for Brian Berns's essay may be a bit harder to reach. Although Iowa farmers would be well aware of the soil erosion problem, Berns fears that they might underestimate its seriousness. His strategy is to appeal to the farmers' economic self-interest, citing research from the USDA that both emphasizes the dimensions of the problem and establishes the credibility of his proposed solutions.

Richard Blake's audience is probably aware of problems with the campus food service but they may not be aware of the extent of the dissatisfaction among students. His survey allows him to define the problem more precisely and get at its source. Although he recognizes that the real source of the problem is lack of competition, Blake is wise enough to see that the situation is unlikely to change unless students make their opinions known. The solution he proposes is a simple one, but far from simplistic. In calling for students to act on their complaints, he is taking on the difficult role of community organizer.

Wheelchair Hell: A Look at Campus Accessibility

■   ■   ■

Shannon Long

University of Kentucky
Lexington, Kentucky

It was my first week of college, and I was going to the library to meet someone on the third floor and study. After entering the library, I went to the elevator and hit the button calling it. A few second later the doors opened, I rolled inside, and the doors closed behind me. Expecting the buttons to be down in front, I suddenly noticed that they were behind me — and too high to reach. There I was stuck in the elevator with no way to get help. Finally, somebody got on at the fourth floor. I'd been waiting fifteen minutes. 1

I'm not the only one who has been a victim of inaccessibility. The University of Kentucky currently has twelve buildings that are inaccessible to students in wheelchairs (Karnes). Many other buildings, like the library, are accessible, but have elevators that are inoperable by handicapped students. Yet, Section 504 of the Rehabilitation Act of 1973 states that 2

> No qualified handicap person shall, because a recipient's facilities are inaccessible to or unusable by handicapped persons, be denied the benefits of, be excluded from participation in, or otherwise be subjected to discrimination under

99

any program or activity receiving Federal financial assistance (Federal 22681).

When this law went into effect in 1977, the University of   3
Kentucky started a renovation process in which close to a
million dollars was spent on handicap modifications (Karnes).
But even though that much money has been spent, there are
still many more modifications needed. Buildings still inaccessible to wheelchair students are the Administration Building, Alumni House, Barker Hall, Bowman Hall, Bradley Hall,
Engineering Quadrangle, Gillis Building, Kinkead Hall, Miller
Hall, Safety and Security Building, and Scovell Hall (Transition).

So many inaccessible buildings creates many unnecessary   4
problems. For example, if a handicapped student wants to
meet an administrator, he or she must make an appointment
to meet somewhere more accessible than the Administration
Building. Making appointments is usually not a problem, but
there is still the fact that able-bodied students have no problem entering the Administration Building while handicapped
students cannot. Though handicapped students can enter the
Gillis Building, they cannot go above the ground floor and
even have to push a button to get someone to come downstairs
to help them. Finally, for handicapped students to get counseling from the Career Planning Center, they must set up an
appointment to meet with someone at another place. In this
case, some students might not use the Center's services
because of the extra effort involved (Croucher).

Even many of the accessible buildings have elevators, water   5
fountains, and door handles that are inoperable by handicapped students (Karnes). Elevators in the Library and Whitehall Classroom Building, for instance, have buttons too high
for wheelchair students, forcing them to ask somebody else to
hit the button. If there is nobody around to ask, the handicapped person simply has to wait. In the Chemistry and
Physics Building, a key is needed to operate the elevator, forcing wheelchair students to ride up and down the hall to find
somebody to help. Many water fountains are inaccessible to
people in wheelchairs. Some buildings have only *one* accessible

water fountain. Finally, hardly any buildings have doorknobs that students with hand and arm impairments can operate.

Many residence halls, such as Boyd Hall, Donovan Hall, Patterson Hall, and Keenland Hall, are also completely inaccessible. If a handicapped student wanted to drop by and see a friend or attend a party in one of these dorms, he or she would have to be carried up steps. Kirivan and Blanding Towers have bathrooms that are inaccessible. Also, in Kirivan Tower the elevator is so small that someone has to lift the back of the chair into the elevator. The complex lowrises—Shawneetown, Commonwealth Village, and Cooperstown Apartments—are also inaccessible. Cooperstown has some first floor apartments that are accessible, but a handicapped student couldn't very well live there because the bathrooms are inaccessible. All eleven sororities are inaccessible, and only five of the sixteen fraternities are accessible. Since the land sororities and fraternities are on is owned by U.K., Section 504 does require that houses be accessible (Transition 14, 15). 6

With so many U.K. places still inaccessible, it is obvious that hundreds of modifications need to be done. According to Jake Karnes, the Assistant Dean of Students and the Director of handicap Student Services, "It will probably take close to a million dollars to make U.K. totally accessible." U.K.'s current budget allows for just $10,000 per year to go toward handicap modification (Karnes). If no other money source is sought, the renovation process could be strung out for many years. 7

A possible solution could be the use of the tuition. If only $2 could be taken from each student's tuition, there would be almost $50,000 extra per semester for handicap modification. Tuition is already used to pay for things ranging from teacher salaries to the funding of the campus radio station. This plan could be started with the beginning of the 1990 Fall semester. The money could be taken from each of the existing programs the tuition now pays for, so there would be no need for an increase in tuition. Also, this would not be a permanent expense because with an extra $50,000 a semester, all of the needed modifications could be finished in ten years. After that, the amount taken from the tuition could be lowered to fifty cents to help cover upkeep of campus accessibility. This 8 plan is practical—but more important, it is ethical. Surely if part of our tuition goes to fund a radio station, some of it can be used to make U.K. a more accessible place. Which is more important, having a radio station to play alternative music or having a campus that is accessible to all students?

June 1980 was the deadline for meeting the requirements of Section 504 (Robinson 28). In compliance with the law, the University of Kentucky has spent close to a million dollars making its campus more accessible. But there are still many more changes needed. These changes will take a lot of money, but if two dollars could be used out of each student's tuition, the money would be there. Handicapped students often work to overachieve to prove their abilities. All they ask for is a chance, and that chance should not be blocked by high buttons, heavy doors, or steps.

9

Works Cited

Croucher, Lisa. "Accessibility at U.K. for Handicapped Still Can Be Better." *Kentucky Kernal*. Date unknown.

Federal Register. Volume 42 (4 May 1977):22681.

Karnes, Jake. Personal Interview. 17 Oct. 1989.

Robinson, Rita. "For the Handicapped: Renovation Report Card." *American School & University* (Apr. 1980):28.

University of Kentucky—Transition Plan. [report]. Date unknown.

Handling the Pressure

. . .

J. Chad Friesen

University of Oklahoma
Norman, Oklahoma

Most everyone is aware of the academic stresses that fall   1
upon new college freshmen; the drastic change in the level of
curriculum and the academic setting can be overwhelming.
However, other potentially damaging types of stress are too
often ignored, overshadowed by the constant concern for aca-
demics. The several types of emotional stress new college students face can have detrimental—and damaging—impact.

The first major new stress falling comes from the sudden   2
change of environment. After eighteen years of living in a
secure, stable home setting, students find themselves in a
strange, "parentless" place. Having to eat, sleep, study, and live
with people you've never met before can be quite scary. For the
people lucky enough to get cooperative roommates, the transition is usually quick and free of major problems. However,
many students are not so fortunate.

Learning self-discipline can also be a major hurdle to over-   3
come. Suddenly, there is no one to say when to study, when to
play and when to go to bed. Almost everyone will agree that it's
nice not to be told constantly what to do, and it is. But, whether
it's admitted or not, there are times when that security is missed.
Students who "mess up" have nobody else to blame but them-

103

selves. For students with problems handling self-discipline, the first semester of college can be disastrous.

    With college and adulthood also comes the need to worry about money more than ever before. The cost of getting a college degree these days is enormous — and still rising. It is a situation that demands careful budgeting strategies. Some parents retain this responsibility and money is obviously of more concern to some students than others. But, almost every student will have some share of financial dilemmas.   4

    Upon graduation from high school, a lot of students are separated from friends they've known for years. This separation, compounded by the absence of parents, can make the first semester a lonely one. Even with new friends, it's not always the same. The third Friday night alone in a dorm room watching television can take a toll on a person's self-esteem.   5

    The ways of coping with these stresses are often far from healthy. All too many students turn to alcohol and drugs. Others try to hold their stresses inside and risk the possibility of going to pieces. A frightening number of students choose the horribly final "solution" of suicide.   6

    Some would deny that the problem is at a dangerous level. Some even say that "it is all in the students' heads." But, the facts are hard to ignore. In Walter Tower alone, there have allegedly been two suicide attempts, one alcohol overdose, and a nervous breakdown. And those are just the incidents I have personally heard about since the beginning of school.   7

    Students at the University of Oklahoma appear to have different views on the subject of emotional stress. When I asked several students if they thought emotional stress was a significant problem at OU, I got various responses. Rob Duerr, freshman, replied, "Yes, I think it affects our ability to function as well as we can, both in and out of school." Marci Sterkel, another freshman, said, "Definitely, everyone I know is screwed up. We all get depressed and manic and just stay in our rooms." Some had slightly different opinions. "I think everyone has stress; it's just how you deal with it that decides whether it's a problem or not," said sophomore Chris Brown. John Wampler, freshman, seemed to agree: "It's a definite problem for   8 some people, but it doesn't bother me because I don't take anything seriously."

Many people feel that OU already deals with these problems adequately, offering a hotline, a counseling service, and a few pamphlets and seminars on various stress-related topics. This is all good; we're heading down the right path. But, it simply is not enough. 9

We need to let students know that they're not alone, that these kinds of stresses are normal and common. We need to make them realize that there is no shame in asking for help. They need to be informed about how to cope with stress. 10

Academic stresses are very well dealt with by such campus services as tutoring, study groups, help sessions, test files, and so on. Other, nonacademic tensions and problems deserve equal attention. 11

There are several different things that the university can do. For example, it could enlist the help of its Residence Advisors (RA's). All that was basically said at our dorm floor's first meeting was, "Hi, I'm your RA, here's my office hours and here's the rules." Why not require the RA's to talk about some of the problems to expect, situations to prepare for, where to go for help, and how to cope? No one would know these things better than an older student like an RA. Dorm meetings are an excellent opportunity to talk about such things. 12

Then, have follow-up meetings every month or so where people have the opportunity to get problems off their chest. I know from experience that it's easier to talk to friends or at least to people you know than to someone on a hotline or a counselor you've only just met. 13

Also, more could be done in writing. The pamphlets handed out at the beginning of the year ("Number Nyne," "Alcohol Abuse," etc.) are a good idea. However, students get tons of pamphlets the first week of school. They're likely to be lost in the shuffle. It would be better to send them out periodically throughout the year. Maybe include them in a newsletter with articles on dealing with dorm life, strained relationships, separation anxiety, self-discipline, time and money management, etc. The cost of this would be almost nothing. We get a free 14

105

newspaper every day; why not devote one paper a month to these important subjects? Or maybe simply include a newsletter with the paper.

Finally, consider ways of helping students who find themselves alone on the weekend. What do students do when their friends go home for the weekend and they're stuck in the dorm room alone? This is a good chance for depression to set in. We already have the occasional dance or movie party, but attendance is usually low. To change this, we need to throw some variety in — scavenger hunts, dating games, contests — anything for a change and to pull those bored people away from their TV's and pizzas. 15

These suggestions would require little work and even less money. The OU Counseling Center could work in cooperation with the Housing Center Association and the Oklahoma Daily to provide the counseling sessions, newsletters, and entertainment events. 16

These suggestions along with what already exists could possibly help a lot of people. What we're doing is good, but we need to do more. Granted, it may not touch the lives of the majority of students, but if it truly helps a handful of desperate people, wouldn't it be worth it? 17

Iowa's Dirty Problem

■　　■　　■

Brian Berns

Iowa State University
Ames, Iowa

Topsoil helps make Iowa one of the most productive agri-　1
cultural states in the nation. This thin, dark layer, found on the
surface, is the most fertile part of the soil. Before farming
began in Iowa, the topsoil layer on farmland averaged 14 to 18
inches. Today, however, there are only 6 to 8 inches left—a
result of soil erosion (USDA 3:2). Consequently, I believe that
Iowa's farmers *must* take immediate action to stop soil erosion
before the state's agricultural future is ruined.

Soil erosion is defined as "the gradual wearing away and　2
removal of the soil from the surface of the earth by water, wind,
and other forces" (USDA 1:3). In Iowa, the two most common
factors contributing to soil erosion are water and wind.

According to the United States Department of Agriculture,　3
"water running off the land erodes more topsoil than any
other natural force" (USDA 4:3). Soil erosion is caused when
water and debris runs across the land, wearing it away. Ground-
water also contains carbonic acid, which can break rocks and
soil particles down and accelerate the process of erosion.
Ditches or small rills in row-cropped fields, soil deposits in
fencerows and road ditches, and muddy water are all signs of
soil erosion by water.

Soil erosion from wind occurs when the force of wind 4 blowing over the soil is great enough to detach soil particles. Rocks are the main agents in this form of erosion, because their abrasiveness causes them to detach other soil particles as they are blown through the air. Clear evidence of wind erosion is dust in the air and deposits of wind-blown soil in road ditches.

Iowa's farmers must be made aware of the seriousness of 5 the problem. A 1982 study by the United States Department of Agriculture revealed a frightening reality:

> Iowa has the *worst* soil erosion of any state at an average of 9.4 tons of topsoil per acre annually on 26.1 million farm acres. That amounts to 240 million tons or 1/16 of an inch of topsoil yearly! This rate is twice the national average (USDA 4:3).

If it takes approximately 30 years to develop one inch of 6 topsoil "under ideal conditions where erosion is very low" (Cooperative Extension Service 1), Iowa's topsoil is being lost almost twice as fast as it is being produced.

The effects of topsoil losses on crop production have 7 largely been covered up by the use of commercial fertilizers and improved crop varieties. However, there are "signs crop yields are reaching a peak and topsoil will be increasingly important" (USDA 4:4).

Iowa's farmers should also be aware that damages caused 8 by soil erosion do not affect cropland only. Sediment and nutrient runoff causes an estimated 11 million dollars worth of damage to surface water supplies (USDA 4:11). When sediment and nutrient runoff enters surface water supplies, it can lead to excessive plant growth, which lowers the capacity of a body of water, causing over population and stunting of fish. Runoff causes a high turbidity level in city water supplies as well. As a result, money must be spent to treat these water supplies before human use.

The question is, then, what can Iowa's farmers do to stop 9 soil erosion? Some farmers may feel that since they have little control over climate, the soil, and the topography of their farmland, there is nothing they can do to stop soil erosion. However, there are several conservation practices which can be used by farmers in their farming practices to control soil erosion (Cooperative Extension Service 4).

Of the several conservation practices that exist, conservation tillage systems offer probably the best hope for controlling soil erosion on cropland. In conservation tillage systems varying amounts of the previous year's crop residue are left on the surface of the soil. This crop residue helps control soil erosion by slowing the speed of water runoff and protecting the soil from the impact of raindrops and wind. "The more residue left, and the more evenly distributed, the better the soil protection" (USDA 3:5). 10

No-till farming is the most common type of conservation tillage. "No-till farming, leaving all the previous year's crop residue on the surface of the soil reduces soil losses by as much as 90 percent" (USDA 3:3). In no-till farming farmers plant each year's crop while leaving the soil and the previous year's crop residue undisturbed. No-till farming is possibly the most effective way to control soil erosion for two reasons. First of all, it leaves the most crop residue on the soil's surface to protect the soil from erosion. Second, the soil is not left loose and worked up from tillage, making it harder for the soil to be carried away by water or wind. 11

Not only does no-tillage farming effectively control soil erosion, but it also benefits the farmer by lowering yearly costs and increasing yields, therefore increasing yearly profits. The primary reason costs are lowered is that farmers would not be purchasing expensive pieces of tillage equipment. Less money being spent on fuel to perform tillage operations also would lower a farmer's yearly cost. One reason no-tillage farming would bring farmers increased yields is that precious soil moisture would not be lost from tillage operations which expose soil moisture to the air causing it to be dried out. Another reason no-tillage farming brings increased yields is that essential nutrients needed for healthy plant growth would not be lost by erosion. As a result, not only does no-till farming provide farmers with a means of controlling soil erosion on their farmland, but it can also increase their yearly profits. 12

Other commonly used conservation tillage methods   13
include chiseling and disking. These two methods allow
farmers a way of tilling their cropland before planting while
still leaving some crop residue on the surface of the soil to
reduce erosion. "The amount of residue they bury depends on
the number and speed of operations, the depth of tillage, soil
conditions, and conditions of the residues" (USDA 4:5). Since
chiseling and disking leave the soil worked up and susceptible
to erosion, they are not as effective as no-tillage farming.

There are a couple of reasons farmers have not been using   14
conservation tillage systems to control soil erosion on their
farmland. First, many farmers have been unaware that these
systems exist as effective methods of controlling soil erosion.
Second, most farmers are reluctant to change farming practices that they have been using all of their lives. However, if
Iowa's farmers want to continue to have topsoil for farming in
the future, they are going to have to learn to use conservation
tillage systems in their farming operations.

A second soil conservation technique that Iowa's farmers   15
can use to control soil erosion on their farmland is to build
terraces. Terraces are man-made raised strips of land that
reduce the rate of soil erosion on farmland by breaking long
slopes of land into a series of shorter slopes (USDA 1:1). On
these shorter slopes, water does not build up as much speed
and consequently has less power to erode soil away. Terraces
can often be laid out parallel to one another to increase farming efficiency.

The reason few farmers have tried terraces as means of   16
controlling soil erosion on their farmland is that they are relatively expensive to build (Cooperative Extension Service 5).
However, once the initial cost of building the terrace has been
taken care of, terraces can provide an effective way of controlling soil erosion for a long time into the future.

Grass waterways provide Iowa's farmers with a third way of   17
controlling soil erosion on their land. "Grass waterways are
often the best means for carrying concentrated runoff water
from a field while avoiding soil erosion" (USDA 4:3). Seeding
a waterway with grass provides soil with a protective covering
from wind and water, making it virtually impossible for the

soil to be eroded away. Of the many conservation systems, grass waterways are probably used the most by Iowa's farmers to control soil erosion. Nevertheless, Iowa's farmers must continue to use grass waterways to ensure the state's agricultural future is not ruined by soil erosion.

A final conservation system Iowa's farmers can use to control soil erosion on their farmland is contouring. In contouring, farmers farm across the natural slope of their land, instead of up and down it. According to the Cooperative Extension Service, "this practice reduces the velocity of overland water flow and provides excellent erosion control for moderate rainstorms" (5). Farmers are reluctant to use this system of farming because it is generally more time-consuming to farm across the natural slope of the land than farming up and down it. This is because farmers must do their field operations at slower speeds for safety reasons when working parallel to slopes. Farmers must realize, though, that spending a little extra time contouring to control soil erosion is a small price to pay to save Iowa's agricultural future. 18

Iowa's farmers must like immediate action to stop soil erosion on their farmland before the state's agricultural future is ruined. Our cropland topsoil is essential for crop production, and it is being lost twice as fast as it is being produced. The primary factors causing soil erosion in Iowa are wind and water. Even though farmers have little control over the climate, soil, and topography of their farmland, there are several conservation practices that can help to control soil erosion. These conservation practices include conservation tillage, terraces, grass waterways, and contouring. In order to make these conservation systems work, though, farmers *must* use them. 19

Works Cited

Cooperative Extension Service, Iowa State University. *Soil Erosion and the Iowa Soil 2000 Program.* Aug. 1982. Pm-1056 ISUP 80-A2-2145.
United States Department of Agriculture 1. *Cropland Terraces in Iowa.* Soil Conservation Service. Feb. 1983. Iowa Job Sheet 210–1.

Brian Berns

United States Department of Agriculture 2. *Soil Erosion by Water.* Soil Conservation Service. Aug. 1987. Agricultural Information Bulletin 513.

United States Department of Agriculture 3. *Soil Conservation Systems for Iowa Cropland.* Soil Conservation Service.

United States Department of Agriculture 4. *Losing Ground: Iowa's Soil Erosion Menace and Efforts to Combat It.* Soil Conservation Service. 1986:755–016.

Note: USDA publication numbers 1–4 have been applied for purposes of referencing for this paper only.

WSU Dining Facilities

■　■　■

Richard Blake

Wright State University
Dayton, Ohio

When I was a waiter at a local pizza parlor, the area mana- 1
ger would come in once every two weeks and give the restaurant an inspection. He would watch us through the course of
an evening and when the crowds subsided he would gather us
all around and give us our review. At the onset of every debrief-
ing, as they were called among the crew, the first words from
his mouth would always be, "From the moment the customer
enters those doors, his dining experience begins. He will form
an opinion in his mind about us, and it is your job to make
sure that opinion is good! If it isn't, I'll know about it, and then
so will you."

Even though my experiences at that restaurant are a year 2
behind me, whenever I eat out I always keep in mind the customer's opinion—especially when *I* am the customer. When
Wright State students eat at the campus facilities, they form
opinions about their dining experience just as any customer
would, and whether that opinion is good or bad is the responsibility of the food service. Recently I conducted a survey to determine the student opinion of the food service at Wright State.
My purpose was simply to see if the students were satisfied with
the overall performance of Service America, the catering company that handles all of the campus dining facilities.

113

I surveyed fifty students over a period of two days at different times and locations. All of those I surveyed ate at least occasionally at one of the dining facilities. The survey rated such aspects as variety, quality, and taste of the food offered as well as the student's opinion of the prices they paid and overall service they received. The ratings given were initially somewhat mediocre. 3

When rating the food's variety, quality, and taste separately, 67.3 percent rated them as fair, with 13.3 percent rating them as excellent and 19.3 percent rating them as poor. As far as the price of the food was concerned, 54 percent thought it was higher than average while 46 percent thought it was average. No one said it was lower than average. Overall service was viewed as fair by 60 percent, with 20 percent calling it either excellent or poor. 4

These results might lead one to believe that there are no strong student complaints with the food services at Wright State, assuming of course that only an overall rating of fair is considered adequate by both the students and the University. However, as I explored the results further I discovered somewhat different conclusions. Of the individuals surveyed, 56 percent felt strong enough in their opinions, either good or bad, to make comments in the space provided at the bottom of the survey. Seventy-five percent of these comments were negative! 5

What makes these results so important is the fact that such a large number of those surveyed felt strong enough to make comments at all, and that the majority of those comments were negative. Furthermore, those with negative comments accounted for an average of about 40 percent of the fair and average ratings on the overall survey and only about 68 percent of the poor ratings. This means that there is a number of people who have distinct complaints about the food service, but rate it as fair anyway. It is perhaps acceptable in this case then to equate fair ratings with somewhat less than adequate performance on the part of the Wright State food service. 6

So exactly what sort of problems do the students at Wright State have with the food service, and how serious are they? The range of comments I received on my survey was fairly wide, starting with general opinions such as "we're humans, not pigs," 7 to more specific instances of dissatisfaction such as "I have received food . . . more than once . . . with mold on it!" As far as students' overall attitude toward the food service, the comments assumed a similar pattern, from "at least the food is safe" to "do *not* give Service America the 10-year contract." I take such comments as evidence of dissatisfaction with Service America.

The specific complaints I received often dealt with multiple instances of receiving cold food or hard, stale buns on sandwiches, but the two largest categories of discontent were low food quality and slow, unfriendly service. One particular student summed up his feelings by saying, "[The wait] is ridiculous for *fair* food!" So then, if these are the problems what are the causes?   8

Some students may have the answer to that question already. Twelve percent of the negative respondents felt that Service America has a monopoly at WSU. I assert that this monopoly is the reason for their problems with the food service. A monopoly does exist, at least in respect to the dining facilities, since all of the on-campus eaters (Allyn, The Bike, The Ratt and the UC) are controlled by Service America. No matter where students go to eat on campus, their money goes to the same place. There is no competition on campus to threaten Service America's profits, and therefore there is no particular reason for them do better than fair in their performance.   9

The problem, then, is the lack of competition. What are some solutions? One solution might be to change catering companies. There are four catering companies that provide this particular type of service to universities and businesses in the area, including Marriot, ARA, Cardinal, and Service America.   10

This solution is oversimplified at best, considering the real problem doesn't necessarily lie with the company itself, but instead with its motivation for performance. Whatever company came in and took over the reins left by Service America would be in the same position as Service America is now! The new company would have yet another monopoly and would be lacking the same competitive drive to perform that the present establishment does.   11

The next answer would then be to create a competitive market at Wright State. Invite several catering services to put   12

115

up their shingles at Wright State, or even better, forget the catering companies altogether and create a food-court setup like the one at the Dayton Mall. This would create the competitive market needed to keep the various companies on their toes. Every company would be in constant competition with the others, trying to outdo one another in price and service to attract business, and thus profits. It seems almost characteristic of "mall food service operations [to do] everything from tinkering with menus to staging elaborate cross-promotions in order to persuade . . . adults . . . to decide to grab a bite to eat" (Goodman 30). If appealing to consumers were important to compete, students would perhaps get the variety and quality in their meals they don't now have.

However, this utopian view is not feasible for several reasons. The first is that Wright State lacks the room for such a setup, and it is presently involved in so many other projects (such as the Nutter Center and the Theater addition) that it cannot make any accommodations. It would also require a large capital investment by other companies to either build this space themselves or renovate pre-existing (but unavailable) space. Perhaps the major reason why this setup is not feasible lies with the viewpoints of the companies themselves. Wright State is a commuter school, and the largest number of students have their own transportation (RTA riders not considered). The students are then free to travel wherever they want for meals. They are not restricted as are the students of such schools as Ohio State or University of Cincinnati, both primarily residential schools (which, coincidentally, do have mall food-court setups). 13

There are also other major considerations of policy and profit involved. If a company, say McDonalds, was to build within the University, they would be first limiting themselves to only the WSU community at large for patronage and secondly submitting themselves to some control and restrictions by Wright State policy. However, if they build across the street, as they have, they are open to the *entire* community of Fairborn (WSU being a part of that community) and subject only to their own control and restrictions. Most other companies adopt a similar view, and in fact are even advised against 14 setting up shop inside facilities they do not own. Chicago-based restaurant consultant John C. Melaniphy advises clients to "find sites along the peripheries," so that "you can control your own destiny" (Goodman 34).

So then, what is left? Perhaps the most obvious answer will 15 suffice. When I was a waiter, and customers were dissatisfied with something, they did the most natural thing; they complained! That was all that was necessary. The moment a supervisor found out that there was a problem he or she turned to solve that problem in an effort to maintain a good customer opinion. The same is true for Service America!

In an interview with Michael Loprete, Director of Dining 16 Services here at Wright State, I found that Service America is willing to listen to complaints. "I want comments," says Mr. Loprete, who is also a member of the Food Service Advisory Committee, an organization comprising several campus associations to investigate and resolve complaints about the food service. "We are here and accessible," he adds, "we are aware of problems and are attempting to address them . . . that is what the committees are for."

The Food Service Advisory Committee makes itself acces- 17 sible by electing representatives from many student organizations such as Student Government and Handicapped Services and by conducting interviews in the Woods, Hamilton Hall, and dining areas to collect student opinions. All complaints reach the Food Service Advisory Committee, which keeps the complaints on file. In addition there are boxes available in every dining facility for student comments of either displeasure or praise. These boxes are locked and only members of the Food Service Advisory Committee have the key.

The solution to the food service problem at Wright State 18 lies in the hands of the students. They have the power and the right to complain if they feel they are being, as one student so eloquently put it, "glued, screwed, and tattooed!" Instead of complaining to each other (which is quite often as far as many complaints go), students need to make their opinions known to Service America and the Food Service Advisory Committee. Service America's best incentive to do well is the renewal of its contract with WSU. If there is indeed large student dissatisfaction, then Service America's contract is threatened because the quality of the service it provides comes into question. Wright State is a good profitmaker for Service America, and it is an account they don't want to lose, so they will do what they can to keep public opinion high.

Individual complaints can best be handled by the man- 19 agers of the separate units. If you receive food that is cold or a bun that is hard and stale, ask to see the manager and resolve the problem then and there instead of carrying the problem back to your table and grumbling about it. If you receive rude and unfriendly service, or have a complaint that you feel cannot be resolved easily, leave a message in the comment box detailing your complaint or contact your representative in the Food Service Advisory Committee.

Making your opinions known is the best way I know of to 20 resolve any problems that exist between the students and the food service. The students who make their opinions and complaints known will have them resolved in one manner or another, and by solving the students' problems as best they are able, Service America will insure good public opinion and keep its contract. This arrangement is beneficial for both parties involved, and since my results concluded that there is no widespread discontent with the food service, there is no real justification for procedures any more radical than those I have suggested.

Perhaps a monopoly does exist at Wright State in the form 21 of Service America, but it is a monopoly that is ultimately controlled by its patrons, who have the freedom and the power to act on their opinions. The choice for action lies in their hands.

Works Cited

Goodman, Stephanie. "Dinner Is Served—At the Mall." *Adweek's Marketing Week* 24 July 1989:30–34.
Loprete, Michael. Personal Interview. 26 Feb. 1990.

▪ Chapter 8 ▪

Making Evaluations

The criteria by which we evaluate the movies we watch, the magazines we read, the stores we shop in, and the comedians we like are often so deeply embedded in our tastes and attitudes that it's hard to articulate them. In these four essays, the writers have managed not only to identify their criteria but to support their judgments with very specific observations and analyses.

The movie review seems to be a common evaluation assignment, and Scott Hyder does a fine job with his review of *Poltergeist*. Establishing his authority early in the essay with useful background information and detailed references to the movie, he goes on to support his judgment with especially effective comparisons to other horror movies.

Ilene Wolf also uses comparison effectively, though she uses it in a more limited fashion, contrasting the new environmental magazine *Buzzworm* with the more well-known *Sierra*. Wolf's organizational plan seems to be particularly well thought out. She moves from the visual aspects of the two magazines to the content and then to editorial policy, implying that the quality of objectivity is perhaps the most impressive aspect of this new magazine.

In Kim Tweten's evaluation of the Grand Forks Food Co-op, both the criteria for evaluation and the comparative judgments are so well integrated into the essay that the reader may not be aware of them at first. It is this subtlety, this avoidance

119

of a mechanical approach to evaluation, that is one of the particular strengths of this essay. Another is its informal tone, a tone that allows Tweten to move easily between the personal testimony in the seventh paragraph and the more objective reportorial style that characterizes the rest of the essay.

Poltergeist: *It Knows What Scares You*

■   ■   ■

Scott Hyder

University of Arizona
Tucson, Arizona

You are an eight-year-old boy all tucked in for the night.   1
Your little sister is sleeping in the bed next to you. Suddenly,
you hear a crash of thunder, and through the window, you can
see the big, old, growling tree in the lightning. It seems to be,
well, to be making faces at you! But, you are a big boy. Nothing
scares *you*. Nothing at— BANG! WHOOSH! The tree comes to life
as it tumbles through the window, grabbing you with its pulsat-
ing, hairy roots from your bed. As you scream for Mommy, the
closet door slowly opens and an invisible, windlike presence
kidnaps your sister. Your nice, cozy dreamhouse turns into a
living hell. Watch out! "They're hee-re!"

In June of 1982, producer/director/writer Steven Spiel-   2
berg defined "horror" with a new word: *Poltergeist*. At first and
final glance, *Poltergeist* is simply a riveting demonstration of a
movie's power to terrify. It creates honest thrills within the con-
fines of a PG rating, reaching for shock effects and the forced
suspension of disbelief throughout the movie. Spielberg wrote
the story, coproduced it, and supervised the final editing. The
directing credit goes to Tobe Hooper, best known for his cult

shocker *The Texas Chainsaw Massacre*, which probably explains *Poltergeist's* violence and slight crudeness.

Nevertheless, *Poltergeist* cannot be classified in the same 3
horror category with such movies as *A Nightmare on Elm Street*, where a deformed psychotic slashes his victims with razor-edged fingernails. Unlike most horror flicks, *Poltergeist* works! Its success is due to excellent characters, music, and special effects — and to the fact that the story stays within the bounds of believability.

The movie takes place in a suburban housing tract. Steve 4
(Craig T. Nelson) and Diane (JoBeth Williams) Freeling have just purchased a new home when their adorable five-year-old daughter, Carol Anne (Heather O'Rourke), awakes to odd voices coming from the snowy TV screen that Steve falls asleep in front of during the late movie. She calls them the "TV people," and with the help of special-effects producer George Lucas and his "Industrial Light and Magic," these people abduct little Carol Anne, provoking turbulence and misery for this once-happy family.

A mere synopsis simply cannot give a real feeling for the 5
story. As Steve Freeling says to the parapsychologists who have come to see the house, "You have to see it to believe it." Each character possesses a unique personality which contributes to the overall feeling the audience has for the story. The characters are represented to be as normal and American as bologna sandwiches — Dad sells houses, Mom sings along to TV jingles. Spielberg likes these characters, illustrating their go-with-the-flow resilience. When things get suddenly hectic toward the climax, these people can display their fear and anger as well as surmise their inner strengths. This is particularly evident when Tangina, the parapsychologist the Freelings hire, instructs Diane to lie to her daughter in order to lure Carol Anne into the light and save her.

"Tell her to go into the light," Tangina instructs. "Tell her 6
that *you* are in the light!"

"No," Diane replies with betrayed emotions. 7

Tangina immediately puts everything into the proper 8
perspective. "You can't choose between life and death when

we're dealing with what's in between! Now tell her before it's too late!"

Such scenes clearly illustrate that Spielberg's characters are, in a sense, the ordinary heroes of the movies.   9

A horror movie, however, cannot rely on terror, anger, and   10
disbelief and hold its audience for two hours. Something needs to accompany these emotions, equally expressing the full extent of the characters' fear and anger. Music composer Jerry Goldsmith contributes his share of eeriness with his Academy-Award-winning soundtrack. The basic theme is a lull-a-bye (entitled "Carol Anne's Theme") that soothes the watcher, providing a cheerful, childlike innocence to the picture. The inverse is the ghost music that accompanies the abduction of Carol Anne and forces our stomachs to writhe. The music brings a straining, vibrating tone that is responsible for 60 percent of the audience's terror. When the clown doll's hand wraps around Robbie's (Oliver Robbins) neck, the sudden blaring of Goldsmith's orchestra is what makes viewers swallow their stomachs. Without it, the scene would never slap our face or give our necks a backward whiplash. Goldsmith matches the actions and emotions of the characters with the corresponding instrumental music, enabling the audience to parallel their feelings with those delivered on the screen.

If a horror movie has a well-developed plot with superior   11
actors and an excellent score to accompany their emotions, then it should be a sure winner at the box office, right? Looking back at such movies as *Rosemary's Baby, The Exorcist*, and the original *Psycho*, one would obviously agree. *Poltergeist*, however, doesn't stop here. It goes even further by providing its audience with a special treat. With the help of *Star Wars* creator George Lucas, Spielberg and Hooper whip up a dazzling show of light and magic. There's an eerie parade of poltergeists in chiffons of light marching down the Freelings' staircase to the climactic scene as a huge, bright, nuclear-colored mouth strives to suck the Freeling children into their closet. Hooper's familiarity with film violence surfaces in a grotesque scene in which one of the parapsychologists hallucinates that he is tearing his face. Such shocking, hair-raising scenes as this make a

huge contribution to horrifying the audience. Many horror films never achieve such reactions. *Poltergeist's* precise timing with such effects makes it completely unpredictable as far as what is to come. From the first sign of a ghostlike hand jumping out of the TV to the staggering scene of dead bodies popping out of the half-dug swimming pool, the special effects team draws every bit of energy out of the audience, dazzling them and forcing them to believe in the horror on the screen.

There have been many movies that possess superior ratings in all of the above. Such movies as John Carpenter's *The Thing* and David Croneberg's *Scanners* won raves for superior acting, background music, and special effects. Why was *Poltergeist* accepted at the box office more than other such movies? Every movie is forced to set up boundaries of believability through certain actions and concepts, and at one point these boundaries will be accepted by the viewer. In *Indiana Jones and the Temple of Doom*, Spielberg created distinguished boundaries in which Indiana Jones defined his heroic stunts. Spielberg, however, unfortunately crossed his boundaries during a scene in which Indiana Jones jumps from one track to another with a moving train cart. From previous observations of Indiana Jones's capabilities, the audience is unable to accept this, nodding their heads with a "give me a break" expression. [12]

In *Poltergeist*, Spielberg and Hooper remain within their established boundaries. Unlike most horror movies that have unfeasible killers who are incapable of dying or monsters that pop out of people's stomachs, *Poltergeist* focuses on the supernatural — a subject with *very wide* boundaries. Because of our lack of knowledge in the area, we are "at the mercy of the writers and directors," as Alfred Hitchcock has phrased it. The boundaries can be greater than most horror movies because of *Poltergeist's* subject matter. The characters' disbelief of their surroundings encourages the audience to accept what is in front of them. Hence, *Poltergeist* successfully stays within its limits, taking them to their maximum, but luring the audience to believe the situation the characters are involved with. [13]

Poltergeist reflects a lot of the fears that most of us grow up with: seeing scary shadows from the light in your closet, mak- [14]

ing sure your feet are not dangling over the bed, forming scary images of the objects in your room. As Spielberg's *E.T.* reminisces about our childhood dreams, *Poltergeist* surfaces our childhood nightmares. With its characters, music, and special effects, and its clearly distinguished boundaries of belief, *Poltergeist* is able to capture its audience with its unique thrills, allowing viewers to link their most inner-locked fears to those on the screen. *Poltergeist*: It knows what scares you!

Buzzworm:
The Superior Magazine

■   ■   ■

Ilene Wolf

University of California at San Diego
La Jolla, California

Many people today exist within their environment without 1
really knowing anything about it. If this ignorance continues,
we will undoubtedly destroy the world in which we live. Only
by gaining a better understanding of our planet, will we be
able to preserve our fragile environment from pollution,
hazardous waste, endangerment of species, and ravaging of the
land. A new magazine is dedicated to enlightening the general
public about these important issues. It is called *Buzzworm*.

What makes *Buzzworm* superior to other magazines deal- 2
ing with the same subject, is that it not only fully explores all
of the aspects of the environment, but it does so in an objective
manner. *Buzzworm* effectively tackles the controversial question of how to best protect our planet and conveys the information in a way that all audiences can understand. In fact, the
term "buzzworm," borrowed from the Old West, refers to a
rattlesnake. The rattlesnake represents an effective form of
communication, for when it rattles or buzzes it causes an
immediate reaction in those who are near. Thus the purpose
of *Buzzworm* is to create a reaction in its readers regarding the
conservation and preservation of the environment.

126

Buzzworm: *The Superior Magazine*

One of *Buzzworm's* most striking features is its visual 3 appeal. Excellent photographs complement the articles. Contrasted with the photography in *Sierra*, another environmental magazine, the superb photographs in *Buzzworm* only seem more striking. The Summer 1989 issue of *Buzzworm* features a dramatic full-page color picture of the grey wolf, which catches the reader's eye and draws attention to the article concerning the endangerment of the grey wolf's habitat. The current issue of *Sierra* also has a picture of the grey wolf, yet it is not only smaller but the colors are not as clear—resulting in a less effective picture. Whereas both photographs of the animal pertain to their corresponding articles, it is the one in *Buzzworm* that makes the reader stop and discover the plight of the grey wolf.

Not only must a photograph be of excellent quality but it 4 also must be placed correctly in the layout to enhance the article. The reader should be able to look at the picture and receive some information about the article it corresponds to. *Buzzworm's* pictures of the East African Masai convey specific information about the tribe. Startling photographs depict the Masai in their traditional dress, focusing on the elaborate beadwork done by the women and the exquisite headdresses worn by the warriors. Looking at one picture of a young warrior wearing a lion's mane headdress, the reader gets a sense of the importance of the ritual and of the great respect that is earned by becoming a warrior. Another picture depicts a mother intently watching her daughter as she learns the art of beading. The look on the woman's face displays the care that goes into the beadwork, which has been an important part of their heritage for many generations. Thus, even before reading the article about the Masai, readers have some understanding of their culture and traditions.

Another functional and informative aspect of *Buzzworm's* 5 layout is the use of subfeatures within an article. A subfeature functions in two ways, first by breaking up the monotony of a solid page of print, and second by giving the curious reader additional information. An article in the current issue entitled "Double Jeopardy" gives the reader an option of learning more about the subject through two subfeatures. The article itself describes the detrimental effects that excessive whale-watching and research are believed to have on the humpback whale. To find further information about what might be contributing to the already low numbers of the humpback whale, one can read the subfeature, "Humpback Whale Survival." Furthermore, for the reader who is not familiar with the subject, there is a second subfeature entitled "Natural History," which gives general information about the humpback whale. No such subfeatures can be found anywhere in *Sierra*.

In addition to being an effective way of adding pertinent information to the article, the subfeatures also add to the unity of the magazine. The subfeatures in *Buzzworm* all share a common background color of grey, adding to the continuity in layout from one article to the next. This produces a cleaner, more finished, and visually appealing magazine. 6

Once again, *Buzzworm* shows superior layout design in keeping the articles from being overrun by advertisements. I realize that ads do generate necessary revenue for the magazine, but nothing is more annoying than an article constantly interrupted by ads. *Buzzworm's* few ads are all in the back of the magazine. In fact, not once does an ad interrupt an article. On the other hand, *Sierra* is filled with advertisements that are allowed to interrupt articles, which only frustrates the reader and detracts from the article. 7

Buzzworm is unique in that it focuses on more than just one aspect of the environment. In contrast, *Sierra* devoted its entire September/October issue to one subject, the preservation of the public lands in the United States. Although it is a topic worthy of such discussion, readers prefer more variety to choose from. The content of *Buzzworm* ranges from the humpback whale to the culture of the Masai to a profile of three leading conservationists. The great variety of issues covered in *Buzzworm* makes it more likely to keep the reader's attention than *Sierra*. 8

Buzzworm's ability to inform the reader is not limited to the information in its articles. Captions also play a large part. Readers who are too lazy to read an entire article most often will look at the pictures and read the captions. Thus *Buzzworm's* long and detailed captions are like miniature paragraphs, giving out more details than the terse captions in *Sierra*, usually 9 consisting of only a few words. The difference in the amount of information in the two magazines is obvious from a look at a typical caption in *Buzzworm*, "Finding relaxation of a different kind, Earthwatch participants spend a vacation patrolling beaches and assisting female turtles in finding a secluded nesting area" compared to one in *Sierra*, "Joshua tree with Clark Mountain in background." Both captions give a description of their corresponding pictures, but only the caption found in *Buzzworm* gives any indication of what the article is about. The captions in *Buzzworm* supplement the articles, whereas the captions in *Sierra* only give brief descriptions of the pictures.

Finally, *Buzzworm* is objective, a rare quality in environ- 10 mental magazines. An article on tourism versus environmental responsibility focuses on both the environmental and economic aspects of tourism, stating that while tourism generates income, it often destroys places of natural beauty that are so often visited. In contrast to this point of view, the article also cites examples where tourism has actually helped to preserve the environment. For every argument presented in *Buzzworm*, the counterargument is also presented. This balance is important, for readers must have all of the facts to be able to make well-informed judgments about controversial issues.

Despite all of its wonderful aspects, *Buzzworm* does have 11 its flaws. Some of its graphics pale next to the color photographs. Also, the photograph sizes should be varied more in size to create a visually more appealing layout. Except for these minor flaws, *Buzzworm* achieves its goal of appealing to its readers. In informing the general public about conservation and protection of our environment, *Buzzworm*, is far more effective than *Sierra*.

Good Food, Good People

■　■　■

Kim Tweten

University of North Dakota
Grand Forks, North Dakota

In the sixties health-food stores came into vogue and achieved a certain following by offering healthful foods with foreign-sounding names. Things like dried kelp, yogurt, and tofu were some of the items being consumed by hippies and other health-food nuts. 1

You might say that the Grand Forks Food Co-op is a spin-off of those first stores. However, the world has changed a lot since the sixties, and the Co-op no longer caters to a small select group of customers. Almost everyone is becoming aware of the importance of health and fitness and the foods they consume. More and more people are reading labels, staying away from nitrates, cholesterol, and other things they can't pronounce. 2

The Co-op has a variety of ways to inform new customers of its existence. It has high visibility at occasions such as Summerthing, Winterthing, Riverboat Days, and other Park Board events. The Co-op almost always wins a ribbon at the Potato Bowl Parade with its Kazoo Band entry and the healthful treats it offers such as fruit leather and Mountain Spring soda pop. Other ways newcomers find out about the Co-op are from ads in the UND student paper and the "Food Facts" column in the 3

Tri County Press publication. Both offer discount coupons for members and nonmembers.

Although the store is not in a well-traveled area, you can   4
find it by following casual directions, such as "turn left at Judy's Tavern, go past J. B.'s Tasty Freeze, then head back east when you get to Jerry's Hair Place." However, it would probably be easier to just look for the big sign on North Washington that points the way to 1602 9th Avenue North. Once you get inside the Co-op, it is easy to rationalize going out of your way to get there.

It's a store that tickles your senses. Unlike huge super-   5
duper markets, it smells great. Tea, herb, and honey flavors fill the air. Although there are no fluorescent lights row after row like at Albertsons, it is a bright, cheery store with all sorts of aesthetically pleasing sights. Well-tended plants and other personal touches make a person feel welcome. There is usually KFJM public-radio music playing softly in the background, several steps up from the elevator music at Hugo's.

Everything in the store is organized and easy to locate. In   6
one corner is a small area for kids to play as parents shop. At the back of the store is a freezer/cooler section displaying everything from goat cheese to yogurt bars. The rest of the space is devoted to a combination of things that you would expect a health-food store to contain, such as bulk nuts, beans, pasta, and flours, as well as a lot of things you might have never expected to see there, like pizzas, snack items, chips, and quick-to-prepare mixes.

A wide variety of people belong to the Co-op—from senior   7
citizens to university students. Some take advantage of the working member discounts while others just enjoy the shopping benefits offered. For $5 a year you receive the *Garlic Press*, a monthly newsletter which highlights store inventory, policies, and people. The April 1989 issue told us about the new fruit-buying club that was formed in response to Alar concerns, the "Think Green" member contest for the month, and new products. It is a newsy, friendly publication that fills you in on other members' special events (births, weddings, travels) as well as updates on food, nutrition, and recipes. Your member-

131

ship also allows you to vote and serve on committees within the Co-op such as Collective Energies.

To our family, the Co-op is an obvious alternative to the glitzy, overcrowded markets where we used to shop. I have grown increasingly fond of the personal service, friendly atmosphere, and fairly wide variety of wholesome natural foods. We're not food fanatics at our house; we eat more junk than we should. We drink Coca Cola after our daughter is in bed and occasionally pig out on Ding Dongs, but in general we try to follow our instincts about the four basic food groups and not give ourselves cancer or high blood pressure while doing so. The Co-op helps us do this. The fact that the Co-op has over five hundred members indicates that it fits other people's lifestyles as well. 8

Granted, there are things that aren't perfect at the Co-op. It's a little off the beaten path; there is no in-house baker, let alone butcher; and the candlestick maker lives in Duluth. There are no double coupons or cute carryout boys available, and some things are just not offered, but it's a store that grows on you the more you shop there. 9

The Co-op is located in a little brick building on the corner of 9th and 16th Street in a quiet residential neighborhood. There is parking out front for five or six cars and an equal number of bicycles. Although the location is quaint and cozy, it is miles from any mall and nowhere near a main drag. This might be a hindrance for any new shoppers or people not willing to go out of their way for groceries. According to manager Caroline King, this is an issue with which the Board is constantly struggling. Should the store move in order to be more visible? The answer for now seems to be expanding the advertising focus so that the widest number of people possible are aware of the store's existence, its contents, and its location. 10

All in all, the Grand Forks Co-op is a wonderful place to be a part of. I often think of Garrison Keillor and Ralph's Pretty Good Grocery when I'm at the Co-op. Like Ralph says, "If we don't have it, you can probably get along without it." 11

Chapter 9

Speculating About Causes

The most obvious common factor in these four essays is that they have been researched and formally documented. Although this is not a necessary feature of this kind of writing, it is clearly desirable, first to document the fact that there is a trend, then to consider what its causes might be.

In Shari Beardslee's essay, the fact that there is a nursing shortage is established immediately in the first paragraph. After that, Beardslee considers two factors that may contribute to the shortage and then goes on to explore in more depth what she sees as the two major causes of the trend. Throughout the essay, she effectively buttresses her argument with information obtained from recent periodicals.

Reese Mason's subject is not so much a trend as a phenomenon. Although he centers his essay on the death of college basketball star Hank Gathers, his broader interest is in "the popularity and importance of the game of basketball among the urban poor." Here there is not the same need for documentation as in Beardslee's essay. Readers are aware of the phenomenon, and Mason can speculate about its causes without too much recourse to facts, statistics, or authority. Still, the statistics in paragraph 5 lend credence to his argument, and at the same time force us to see that this is not so much a trivial phenomenon as part of a larger social pattern.

It is one of these large social patterns that Deena Mallareddy analyzes in "Decreasing Democracy." Like Beardslee,

133

Mallareddy establishes the trend early in her essay, then draws on analysis from experts to explain it. It's worth noting that because the non-voting trend has been in effect for some time now, Mallareddy's sources include not just recent periodicals but academic articles and books devoted to the subject as well.

In Anan Huynh's examination of the causes of "The Increase in College Enrollment Among Asian Americans," another feature of a good causal analysis is evident: the repudiation of competing causal theories. Since some readers may believe that it is Asians' "natural inclination for science and math" that accounts for their high rates of college enrollment, Huynh brings up this point and explains why it is a misconception. Huynh's use of charts to present statistical information in a "reader friendly" format is another notable feature of this essay.

The Need for Nurses

■ ■ ■

Shari Beardslee

Eastern Michigan University
Ypsilanti, Michigan

At one time it was the dream of many little girls to become 1
a nurse. Today, however, America is facing its worst nurse shortage since World War I (Gorman 77). Carolyne Davis, head of
the Health and Human Services Secretary's Commission on
Nursing, estimates that currently about 200,000 nurses are
needed to fill the vacancies (Kleinman 69). The nursing shortage is found everywhere. The Hay Group, a business consult-
ing firm, reports that 60 percent of all hospitals in the United
States have shortages substantial enough to threaten the quality of care provided. The Southeast seems to have the most
severe shortage, an astonishingly high 68 percent (Miller 32).
Even our area is experiencing a shortage of nurses. Seventy-
seven ads for nurses were printed in the April 15, 1990, issue
of the *Detroit News and Free Press*. The ads were nearly begging
for nurses, offering signing bonuses, instant pay, and new
rates. The demand for nurses seems widely spread throughout
the nursing field. Medical, surgical, critical care, obstetrics,
and nursery nurses alike are all becoming rare commodities.

What has become of these women in white? The answer 2
lies in not one but several causes. One possibility is the fact
that women have greater career options. In the past, women
who chose to work outside the home had two basic choices:

135

nursing or teaching. Today, more women than ever are in the work force, but their options have greatly increased. There are women doctors, lawyers, firefighters, and police officers. In fact, women today are found in nearly every field of work. Nursing has been left behind, as women move on to jobs with higher pay and greater status. Nowadays, a career in nursing is socially degrading. A woman (or a man) in this field is often looked down upon as "merely a nurse." Career counselors and teachers may also be at fault. Carolyne Davis spent a year trying to find an explanation for the nursing shortage and was appalled to learn that many high school students are actually being steered away from nursing, told by teachers and counselors that they're "too bright to be a nurse" (Hubbell 73).

Another reason for the nursing shortage is increased   3
demand. Americans are living longer than ever and requiring more medical attention. In fact, the number of elderly patients has almost doubled in the past two decades (Gorman 78). Obviously a larger population requires more nurses. AIDS and other diseases have caused more and more people to need nursing care. Usually, fatal diseases mean long drawn-out hospital stays—which mean more nurses are needed to care for these patients. It is estimated that by the end of the century, the demand for nurses will be double the supply (Will 80).

Although new career options and increased demand are   4
partially to blame, the two greatest factors are low salaries and poor working conditions. The average starting pay for nurses is around $22,500. This is a comparable starting pay for most college graduates. However, the average maximum salary is $32,000—and is usually reached in six to seven years (Hubbell 73). Nurses can expect less than a 40 percent wage increase during their entire career (Will 80). As if low wages were not bad enough, there isn't much to look forward to afterward either. A survey of the American Nurses Association in 1988 revealed that only one quarter of nurses have retirement benefits (Seixas 105). With so little financial reward, the nursing field is hardly appealing.

The intense working conditions of nurses are also rather   5
undesirable. The medical community has come to rely on nurses as cheap, versatile labor. For the amount they're paid, it

would seem that a nurse's job would be fairly simple and relatively stress-free. Nothing could be further from the truth. A nurse must have an abundance of stamina, superior technical know-how, and the ability to withstand a tremendous amount of pressure. Stress may explain the especially high burnout rate. And nurses' responsibilities are constantly increasing due to advances in medical technology.

A new program installed by Medicare is contributing to the difficult working conditions. The Prospective Payment System (PPS) is a program in which hospitals are paid a predetermined fee for each patient—determined by the condition or illness of the patient. If the hospital can provide the care for less, it keeps the difference. If it costs more, the hospital must cover the excess. As a result, hospitals began laying off LPN's, aides, secretaries, clerks, messengers, and housekeepers, which means nurses must often do their own paperwork, take blood samples and specimens to the lab, make beds, and even mop floors. What ever happened to the nurses we used to know—whose job was to care for the sick? The nursing shortage is really a vicious circle. There is a shortage, which causes the existing nurses to work twice as hard to compensate for the lack. This causes them to burn out quicker, causing a greater shortage. And the process repeats—getting worse each time. The turnover rate for nurses is an amazing 45 percent (Miller 33).

Gail Douglas, an operating-room nurse at Atlanta's Northside Hospital, has been a nurse for three decades. She has worked in almost every nursing specialty. Gail is trying to support herself and her three daughters. Last year her earnings totaled $37,116. She has two goals: to keep herself from getting deeper into debt and to change careers. She says she'll do anything but nursing: "It's a dead-end job." Gail is fifty years old and has been trained only for nursing. At her age, it is unlikely that she will be able to pursue a new career. Why is the burnout rate so high? Why are people like Gail so dissatisfied with their jobs? As already mentioned, a nurse's job is extremely difficult. The hours are also undesirable. Nurses often work 50–60 hours per week (Gorman 77). Because of the lack of nurses, those we have must work overtime and extra shifts. With all of

Shari Beardslee

the responsibilities of a nurse, these extra hours can be very trying and extremely stressful. It is no wonder the burnout rate is so high.

The nursing profession is unattractive and unpopular. 8 The opening of new fields for women and an increase in the demand for nurses has created the tremendous shortage. The fact that nurses are overworked and underpaid has also made it an undesirable profession. Given these facts, it is not surprising that there is such a great shortage of nurses today.

Works Cited

Gorman, Christine. "Fed Up, Fearful, and Frazzled." *Time* 131 (14 Mar. 1988):77–78.

Hubbell, John G. "Where Have All the Nurses Gone?" *Readers Digest* 134 (June 1989):71–76.

Kleinman, L. "Code Blue." *Health* 21 (Feb. 1989):68–71, 88.

Miller, Annetta, Elizabeth Bradburn, Betsy Roberts. "Seeking a ℞ for Nurses." *Newsweek* 114 (10 July 1989):32–33.

Seixas, Suzanne. "A Nurse's Battle With Burnout." *Money* 18 (Sept. 1989):104–106.

Will, George F. "The Dignity of Nursing." *Newsweek* 111 (23 May 1988):80.

Basketball and the Urban Poor

．　．　．

Reese Mason

University of California at Riverside
Riverside, California

> For a while there, Gathers had beaten the system, the cycle
> that traps so many black youths in frustration and poverty.
>
> Art Spander

On the evening of March 4, 1990, much like any other night,　1
I sat in my living room fixed to the television as ESPN's Sport
Center broadcast the day's sporting news. The lead story was
about last year's national leader in rebounding and scoring
in collegiate basketball, Loyola Marymount's Hank Gathers.
It was not unusual for Gathers to be in the news, given his
many fantastic performances and displays of great character.
He had become much more than a premier basketball player
since achieving athletic stardom. Yes, Hank Gathers had
become an inspiration to all those who, like himself, had the
misfortune of being born members of the black-American
urban poor. This story, however, was not about a new scoring
record, or a buzzer-beating shot. Nor was it a commentary on
how Hank had not forgotten what community he had hailed
from, and how he intended to move his mother and son out of
poverty when he made it to the "Show." No, this news story was
about a 23-year-old basketball player collapsing and dying on
the court.

139

In utter dismay, I immediately demanded some reason for the unbelievable events. After an incident some three months earlier, Gathers had been tested and found to have cardiomyopathy (a type of arrythmia). How in the world could the doctors have allowed him to continue playing? With such a heart defect, how could he allow himself to continue playing? How could the game of basketball have become more important to Hank Gathers than life itself? The night of March 4 was a sleepless one for this sports fan. I lay awake in restless wonder at what could have compelled a man of my age to risk his life for a game.

The answers came to me the next day in a follow-up story about the tragic death. The piece was a tribute to the life of Hank Gathers. Appropriately, the story began where Hank's life began, and suddenly, with one shot of the camera, I understood. I understood what drove him to greatness on the basketball court. I understood what compelled Hank to continue playing even after he knew he had a heart defect. Like most middle-class sports fanatics, I was well aware that many black athletes come from the slums. I was even aware that Hank Gathers had risen out of a Philadelphia ghetto to achieve greatness in college basketball. Never, though, had I really sat down and considered how growing up in the worst possible scenario could make the game of basketball so popular—and, in Hank Gather's case, as valuable as life itself.

Basketball is popular among the urban poor because it is virtually the only inexpensive path to success available. Unlike football or baseball, basketball requires little money or formal organization to play. All that is needed is a few dollars for a ball and access to a hoop, found at any school or playground. Additionally, it can be practiced and all but perfected on the individual level, without additional players, coaches, or facilities.

Our society offers those who can play basketball well an education that might not otherwise be obtained by the poor. Education is a limited and insufficient resource to the urban poor. There are no easy answers, I admit, but the facts are indisputable. In order to get a quality education, the poor have to win scholarships. Due to its popularity in America, and its college connection, basketball has become one avenue to a higher education. Even when college basketball players are unable to continue playing in the "pros," their university degrees may lead to other good jobs and thus to economic success.

Yet, education is not the motivating factor behind the suc- 6 cess stories of the poor any more than it is among the success stories of the middle class; money is. After all, money is what you are judged on here in America, along with popular recognition. Basketball provides an avenue from the urban ghetto to the highest echelons in America via money and popularity. Hank was honest about what was important to him when he said, "I'm in college to play basketball. The degree is important to me, but not that important."[1] Hank understood that basketball was the vehicle that would take him where he wanted to go. It offered him money (multi-millions, in fact), education, and popularity—the three components of the American Dream.

We recognize Hank Gathers because of his tragic death, 7 but only because he was a fantastic basketball player. It is hard for us to admit, but who would have taken time out for Hank Gathers and his family had he died of a heart defect while playing ball in the Rowand Rosen housing project where his family still lives? Those who were close to him, assuredly, but not the nation. This is why basketball was so important to Hank Gathers, and it may be why he continued playing despite the risk of dying on the court. Hank Gathers' story helps us to see why basketball is so popular among, and dominated by, the urban poor. Basketball is an "E-Ticket" out of the ghetto, one of the best available means of getting nationwide recognition and providing for their family.

Works Cited

Almond, Elliot. "Gathers, Pepperdine's Lewis Had Special Bond." *Los Angeles Times* (7 Mar. 1990):C8.

---

[1]Spander, Art, "The Sporting News," March 19, 1990, p. 5.

Hudson, Maryann and Elliot Almond. "Gathers Suit Asks for $32.5 Million." *Los Angeles Times* (21 Apr. 1990):C1,C20.

Spander, Art. "Who's to Blame for Gathers' Tragic Death?" The *Sporting News* (19 Mar. 1990):5.

Statistical Abstract of the United States 1989, U.S. Bureau of Census, 109th ed., Washington D.C. (1989).

Decreasing Democracy

■   ■   ■

Deena Mallareddy

University of California at San Diego
La Jolla, California

Here's the scenario: A twenty-nine-year-old jockey and 1
truck driver, unmarried, lives with his widowed mother and
sister. One day he is stopped outside a video store for an interview about the upcoming election. The interviewer realizes he
is interviewing the most uninformed man he's ever met. After
a succession of "I don't knows," facts begin to emerge. He says
he is registered to vote, but uninterested in the election and
unsure of voting. In answer to a question about the candidates,
the jockey/truck driver replies, "I don't know nothing about
that. I just vote the way the guy at the corner tells me." Why, asks
the interviewer. "Because he does me favors. I just vote the way
he says."

I don't want to know that people vote like that. Sadly, 2
though, this jockey/truck driver is a better citizen than my golf-
playing, six-figure-salary neighbor across the street. My neighbor doesn't vote at all. He represents a trend that has attacked
the whole of America. The statistics are embarrassing: 64
percent voted in 1968, 57 percent voted in 1974, and by 1984,
only 48.6 percent of those eligible cast votes (Niemi 64). This
decline in voter turnout has drastically weakened American democracy.

143

Deena Mallareddy

The Non-Voter's party is the most rapidly growing party in America, in 1980 and 1984 capturing 51.4 percent of the electorate. George Bush resides in the Oval Office with the explicit support of barely one in four adult Americans. It is a trend that confounds the experts. Positive voter reform in the past 20 years has eliminated voting obstacles—eliminating the poll tax, cracking down on voting rights violations, easing eligibility rules, and lowering the voting age—yet fewer and fewer eligible voters are going to the polls. Voter analyst Curtis Gans estimates that since the reforms 20 million Americans have *joined* the ranks of the non-voters (Judis 20). 3

Non-voters are everywhere. It isn't just the bum on the park bench, nor is it just the 38-year-old manager of the bowling alley. All professions, crafts, classes, and ethnic groups contribute to the slide in voter turnout. 4

The question is, WHY? Political analysts are stumped. A few hypotheses are emerging, however, in the efforts at understanding and reversing the trend. 5

American democracy depends on the power of the individual in the government. Obviously, the government has not communicated this to its citizens; many citizens are convinced that in the end, the government governs the way it wants to. Any sense of actually controlling the national destiny by ballot seems to be fading steadily. More people feel that the link between their vote and public policy is tenuous at best. A study by the National Bureau of Statistics reports that 74 percent of Americans believe life will remain virtually unchanged regardless of whoever wins an election. The implication is that ours is an unresponsive, insensitive government. Consider some answers to a questionnaire sponsored by the Democratic Party: 6

> I don't think public officials care much about what people like me think.... People like me don't have any say about what the government does.... They can't even get my taxes right. (Niemi and Stanley 207)

When politics is controlled by "big interests" which have no concern for the "little folks," people tend to withdraw from politics entirely. An increase in the Non-Voters Party is the result.

144

Government neglect is only one cause. The decrease in   7
voter turnout also rides heavily upon disenchantment with
politics in general. Political figures are failing us emotionally
and morally. We don't have enough fingers to count the scan-
dals: Iran Contra, Ollie North, WedTech. Most nonvoters dis-
miss politics altogether. Says one skilled auto worker, "They're
all crooked. They promise you the world. Then they get in
office and forget all about you. They're too busy shoving their
girlfriends in the closet when the wife comes home" (Judis 18).
Disgusted with loose morals and crime amongst politicians
and their policies, voters reject politics altogether.

Negative campaigning contains all the ingredients neces-   8
sary to sour any election, and turnout decline must be partially attributed to political mudslinging. Any concerned
citizen has to find this "entertainment" repulsive and deroga-
tory to government ideals. Voters anticipate respectful,
focused debates on issues come election time, expecting
politics, not personal attacks. Sadly, campaigning has deter-
iorated to the point of having to be swept off the floor. Looking at the 1988 Bush/Dukakis campaign, I see insults and
flag waving, nose and senility jokes. Negative campaigning
produces the same effects as make-up; excessive powder
wrecks the true texture beneath it. Political analyst Abigail
McCarthy states:

> Throughout the eighties, our politics have been the relation-
> ship of persons to packages . . . packages with human face
> and form, put together by pollsters, image-makers, pulse-
> takers, and speechwriters. Voting under such conditions is
> not making a choice; it is buying a product. (8)

News and issues are trivialized, and voting becomes a mere
joke. What is worse is how long the campaigns keep this up.
Campaigns that begin unprofessionally in the snows of New
England, end unprofessionally in the swelter of summer conventions. By then, candidates have torn each other up so completely that we end up hating all of them. The concerned
citizen recoils. The eventual reaction is to circumvent voting
altogether, thus the decline in voter turnout.

We've come a long way from the days of discriminatory   9
literacy tests and poll taxes, but new legal and structural
requirements still block voter participation. This is yet
another reason for declining voter turnout. Apparently trivial
factors make voter registration difficult. More people, for
example, uproot and move on a regular basis. "Modern
nomads" often want to vote, but give up because they lack the
required permanent address, or because they haven't resided
in a state long enough. Irregular weekday office hours, no
evening or Saturday registration, unpredictable closing dates,
and intimidating 40-page prep booklets are not small incon-
veniences, and they dent the overall voter turnout. As two
experts say:

> Voting in America is not a federal responsibility; it is a mat-
> ter for individual states, each of which has different laws,
> many of them recently more complex with busy work. If all
> states adopted looser provisions, national voter turnout
> would *increase* by nine percent. (Rosenstone and Wolfinger
> 85, italics added)

The decline in party affiliation and party partisanship is   10
the largest factor in the trend. Analyst Shaffer stresses this factor, concluding that "twenty to thirty percent of the decline in
voter turnout results from the decline of partisanship"
(Abramson and Alderich 506). Fewer citizens have steady and
strong psychological identification with a party. Modern party
affiliation is less of a guide to political choices. One out of four
Americans consider themselves strong partisans, while thirty-
eight percent are independent. People are therefore deprived
of a sense of political identity. In the past, political parties
provided clearcut viewpoints, and voters felt a strong allegi-
ance to one side or another. Today's decline in partisanship
directly lowers voter turnout rate. The weakening of partisanship results from the loss of common causes. Parties are gray;
trying to represent everyone has resulted in not representing
anyone. Today's political parties are no longer refuges; and
party affiliation, once the spinal thread connecting citizen
and political processes, is a thread sadly paralyzed. Thus, the

individual is left swirling indecisively, forced to choose alone. As the statistics indicate, the decision is too exhausting and responsible a task to undertake.

Maybe nonvoters would convert over if they discovered 11
their true views or cared to formulate them. Indifference is the frosting on a cake of ignorance and irresponsibility. The nonmotivational factors of our society as a whole perpetuate the lack of participation in our system today. If we all quit casting ballots, we might as well fire George and find another Adolph. We might as well pull the kids from kindergartens because we ultimately do not mind what becomes of them. Voting is, in the end, an act of individuals. The importance of a single vote *does not* depend upon how important people think their votes are. Voting makes democracy possible; democracy is therefore the reward for voting. Some people save whales. I say we save democracy.

Works Cited

Abramson, Paul, and John Alderich. "Decline in the Electoral Participation in America." *American Political Science Review* 76 (1984): 502–521.

Campbell, Angus, Phillip Converse, Warren E. Miller, and Donald E. Stokes. *The American Voter.* New York: John Wiley and Sons, 1983.

"Can't Be Bothered." *The Economist* 309 (22 Oct 1988):17.

Judis, John. "No Place to Go." *The Progressive* 44 (Oct. 1980):18–21.

Kleppner, Paul. *Who Voted?* New York: Praeger, 1982.

McCarthy, Abigail. "Why We Stay Home." *Commonwealth* 108 (16 Jan. 1981):8–9.

Niemi, Richard, and Harold G. Stanley. *Vital Statistics on American Politics.* Washington D.C.: Congressional Quarterly, 1988.

Niemi, Richard, and Herbert Weisberg. *Controversies in American Voting Behavior.* San Francisco: Freeman, 1982.

Recer, Paul. "Why Voters Have a Bad Case of the Blahs." *U.S. News and World Report* 89 (13 Oct. 1980):36.

Rosenau, Jimmy. "Why Americans Don't Vote." *USA Today* 109 (Oct. 1984):3.

Rosenstone, Steven, and Raymond Wolfinger. *Who Votes?* London: Yale University, 1980.

College Enrollment and
Asian Americans

■   ■   ■

Anan Huynh

University of California at San Diego
La Jolla, California

Although Asian Americans total less than 1.6 percent of   1
the total population in the United States they make up 26 percent of the freshmen at University of California, Berkeley,
24 percent at University of California, Los Angeles, 23 percent
at the California Institute of Technology, 17 percent at Stan-
ford, and 15 percent at University of California, San Diego
(Howard, 1988, p. 1). The enrollment of Asian Americans on
college campuses has increased dramatically in the past
decade. As shown in Appendix A, the percentages of the first-
time freshmen enrollment among Asians at University of
California, San Diego, have increased every year since 1984. In
the past five years their enrollment increased an average of
1.64 percent per year while other ethnic groups have gone
down in one year or another.

This increase in Asian American enrollment is due to   2
their great success in high school. As the *Phi Delta Kappa*
reports, Asian American students have become so successful
that they have created a new stereotype in education — the
"model minority" (Divoky, 1988, p. 220). Despite the fact that
many are recent immigrants to the United States, their hard

work and determination have become threatening to other American students. Asian American students are considered the whiz kids of math and science contests. According to Jean Latz Griffin and Mark Zambrano, more than half of the elementary school winners of a Chicago citywide math contest were Asians. Furthermore, a 1987 study shows that Asian American students outscored every other ethnic group, including whites, on the math section of the Scholastic Aptitude Test and the College Board Achievement Examination (Hubler, 1988, p. 1).

As the result of such outstanding achievement, more and more Asian Americans are getting into college. But the real question is what are the reasons for this kind of success? There are numerous reasons, all linked to two factors: family pressure and increasing immigration.

The majority of Asian American students feel pressure to excel in school. Writing from a personal point of view, I am an Asian American who came to the United States at the age of six. Throughout my elementary school years I had mostly American friends, but somehow I was different from them. My parents expected me to come home from school and do homework, while my friends watched television and went out to play. I was expected never to fail, while my friends were expected only to be disciplined in school. At bedtime I was told to work hard in school, while my friends were told a bedtime story. I am not an exception among the Asian American students. We are not allowed to fail. We are the victims of our parents' ignorance, for they do not understand that in the American educational system studying is not the most important thing at school. Often, the only thing they say to their children is "Get me a doctor's degree." Many Asian American students resent the pressure they feel from their parents; nonetheless, they fulfill their parents' wishes and succeed.

Many come from countries where education is for the rich, and so they tend to push their children to take full advantage of the opportunities that are offered in the American educational system. Because education is a pathway to a rich and comfortable life in their native country, Asian parents stress education as a means for their children to obtain more com-

149

fortable lifestyles in the future. Therefore, Asian American students are more likely than other ethnic groups of students to enroll in academic and college preparatory classes: 47 percent of Asian American students enroll in such courses, compared to 37 percent of white, 29 percent of black, 23 percent of Hispanic, and 23 percent of Native American students. Throughout high school, Asian American students earn more total credits than other groups of students. Even in the senior year they maintain a heavier workload and thus are more prepared for college than other groups. The Californian Postsecondary Education Commission reports that Asian high school graduates are twice as likely as white students and six times as likely as blacks and Hispanics to meet the entrance requirement for the state's public universities (Divoky, 1988, p. 220). As a result, more and more Asian students go to college.

It is worth noting also that many Asian families immi- 6
grated to the United States with nothing. Often poor, they have to work hard to make a living. As a result the parents pass on the belief to their children that hard work is the only way to succeed. But why are Asian American students more successful than other ethnic groups, whose parents have also worked hard to battle the same hardship? Historically, most Asians have a long cultural tradition in which education has played a major role. Although few can afford the tuition in their native country, higher education has always been well respected by all social classes. This deep cultural tradition that has been passed on for generations motivates Asian Americans to work hard in the hope that one day their work is going to pay off. Therefore, Asian Americans spend more time on homework than other students. Divoky reports that Asian American high school students in the San Francisco Bay Area spend an average of 11.7 hours a week doing homework, while white students spend only 8.6 hours a week. Because education is their priority, Asian American students are less likely than other ethnic groups to have a part-time job while they are in school. "Only about 24 percent of Asian American students work 15 or more hours per week, as compared to 32 percent of white, 30 percent of black, and 36 percent of Hispanic students" (Peng, 1984, p. 10).

Furthermore, many Asian parents want their children to 7 do better than they did themselves, and so they push them to work hard. They urge their children to look for jobs with high salaries, but they also encourage them to set goals for prestigious careers such as medicine, law, and engineering. As a result, Asian American students have higher educational aspirations than other students. Reports show that about 35 percent of Asian American high school students by their sophomore year have decided to go to school beyond their four-year college degree, as compared to 18 percent of whites, 20 percent of blacks, and 14 percent of Hispanics. Another 30 percent of Asian American students wish to acquire a four-year college degree (Peng, 1984, p. 10). Having such high aspirations so early on means that more and more Asian students enroll in college.

The Asian family structure is quite different from most 8 ethnic groups in the United States. The father is expected to be the head of the household, responsible for providing for the family. He goes to work while the mother often stays home and makes sure the family runs smoothly. In addition to providing for the family, it is the father's, not the mother's, responsibility to monitor the children's performance in school. The father feels dishonor if his children do badly in school. Appendix C shows that there are significantly more Asian fathers monitoring their children's homework than any other race. As Peng points out, this may be a factor in determining students' performance (Peng, 1984, p. 11).

The rising influx of immigrants over the past decade is 9 another important cause of the increasing enrollment. Asian Americans have become the fastest growing minority, making up about 2 percent of the nation's population, up significantly in the last two decades (Divoky, 1988, p. 220). America is known as the land of riches and success, and so many middle-class workers from Hong Kong, the Philippines, South Korea, and Taiwan come hoping to fulfill their dreams. And to the Vietnamese, America stands for the land of freedom. The Vietnam War ended in 1975, which marked another peak of Asian immigration. Many of these immigrants soon found out that acquiring a new culture, language, and country brings many hardships. Oftentimes, they have to work menial jobs for mini- mum wage. Such parents want to ensure that their children go to college, to keep them from going through similar hardships. The increase in college enrollment among Asian Americans has only been apparent in the last few years because these children have just reached college age.

Many people believe that this increasing enrollment is due   10 to Asians' natural inclination for math and science. Although some Asian American students are gifted in these fields, there are as many gifted students in other races too. The misconcep- tion of Asian Americans being smarter in math and science has come from their winning all the math and science contests and getting high scores on the Scholastic Aptitude Test. How- ever, the real reason is that many Asian Americans are recent immigrants from countries where math and sciences are stressed. In addition, they often have difficulty with English so they see math and science as an opportunity to succeed with minimum language skills (Howard, 1988, p. 1).

Family pressure and the increased inflow of immigrants   11 are the two underlying causes of increased college enrollment among Asian Americans. As the number of recent immigrants coming to the United States increases, the number of Asian students pressured to go to college also increases. Their high achievement seems to reaffirm their parents' values of commit- ment and hard work. What they sacrifice seems to motivate them to work hard for the future. However, are their sacrifices too high to pay? Many researchers have found that Asian Americans are forced to grow up without having a childhood. They are put under heavy pressure to be the "perfect student," and to fulfill their parents' wishes. Maybe someday the parents and students both will realize that the perfect student is not always the one who gets all A's.

Works Cited

Divoky, Diane. "The model minority goes to school." *Phi Delta Kappa.* Nov. 1988, p. 219–225.

Griffin, Jean and Zambrano, Mark. "Weight of excellence on Asians." *Chicago (Illinois) Tribune*, 23 June 1986: p.1.

Howard, Marjorie. "Asians fighting." *Boston (Massachusetts) Herald*, 22 May 1988: p. 1.

Hubler, Shawn. "Even pre-teens feel pressure to make the grade for college." *Los Angeles (California) Herald Examiner*, 22 May 1988: p. 1.

Peng, Samuel. *School experiences and performance of Asian American high school students.* Apr. 1984: p. 1–46.

Anan Huynh

Appendix A
Freshman Enrollment by Ethnicity

Four ethnic groups (Chicanos, Latinos, Filipinos, and Asians) experienced enrollment increases despite the overall decline in the size of the new freshman class. Blacks and Native Americans, however, experienced substantial decreases (– 30% and – 29%, respectively). New freshman enrollment among whites was down 13% from the previous year. Proportionately, whites represent 57.7% of the total freshman population, students of color represent 35.7%, and students for whom ethnicity is unknown represent 6.6%.

Ethnicity	1984	1985	1986	1987	1988	1989	1988/89
Black	88	83	97	76	94	66	– 30%
	(3.5%)	(3.6%)	(3.4%)	(3.0%)	(3.0%)	2.4%)	
Chicano	144	136	154	168	204	206	+ 01%
	(5.6%)	(5.8%)	(5.4%)	(6.6%)	(6.9%)	(7.5%)	
Latino	37	62	74	72	96	101	+ 05%
	(1.4%)	(2.7%)	(2.6%)	(2.8%)	(3.3%)	(3.7%)	
Filipino	104	129	163	186	87	90	+ 03%
	(4.1%)	(5.5%)	(5.7%)	(7.3%)	(3.0%)	(3.3%)	
Native	13	13	10	19	31	22	– 29%
American	(0.5%)	(0.6%)	(0.3%)	(0.8%)	(1.1%)	(0.8%)	
White	1,697	1,498	1,742	1,542	1,825	1,580	– 13%
	(66.7%)	(64.0%)	(60.8%)	(60.8%)	(62.1%)	(57.7%)	
Asian	302	303	433	371	452	495	+ 10%
	(11.9%)	(13.0%)	(15.1%)	(14.6%)	(15.4%)	(18.1%)	
Other	160	99	192	103	147	180	+ 22%
	(6.3%)	(4.3%)	(6.7%)	(4.1%)	(5.0%)	(6.6%)	
Total:	2,545	2,323	2,865	2,537	2,936	2,740	– 07%
	(100%)	(100%)	(100%)	(100%)	(100%)	(100%)	

Appendix B
Total Undergraduate Enrollment by Ethnicity

The ethnic breakdown of UCSD's undergraduate population appears in Table 4UG. Between 1988 and 1989, greater than average enrollment gains occurred among Native American (+ 16%), Latino (+ 13%), Asian (+ 8%), and Chicano (+ 8%) students. Only Filipino, black, and white students experienced enrollment declines (− 8%, − 6%, and − 1%, respectively).

Ethnicity	1984	1985	1986	1987	1988	1989	1988/89
Black	308	341	385	402	415	390	− 06%
	(2.6%)	(2.8%)	(2.9%)	(3.0%)	(2.9%)	(2.7%)	
Chicano	561	614	664	741	825	887	+ 08%
	(4.8%)	(5.1%)	(5.1%)	(5.5%)	(5.8%)	(6.2%)	
Latino	204	258	289	328	401	453	+ 13%
	(1.7%)	(2.1%)	(2.2%)	(2.4%)	(2.8%)	(3.2%)	
Filipino	421	480	584	685	659	607	− 08%
	(3.6%)	(4.0%)	(4.5%)	(5.0%)	(4.7%)	(4.2%)	
Native	52	52	53	67	95	110	+ 16%
American	(0.5%)	(0.4%)	(0.4%)	(0.5%)	(0.7%)	(.8%)	
White	7,959	8,069	8,552	8,719	8,892	8,839	− 01%
	(68.0%)	(66.0%)	(65.3%)	(64.2%)	(63.0%)	(61.7%)	
Asian	1,307	1,495	1,756	1,868	2,010	2,171	+ 08%
	(11.2%)	(12.4%)	(13.4%)	(13.7%)	(14.3%)	(15.2%)	
Other	888	801	811	779	808	867	+ 07%
	(7.6%)	(6.6%)	(6.2%)	(5.7%)	(5.7%)	(6.0%)	
Total:	11,700	12,110	13,094	12,589	14,105	14,324	+ 02%
	(100.0%)	(100.0%)	(100.0%)	(100.0%)	(100.0%)	(100.0%)	

Appendix C
Percentage of Students Reporting that Their Mother and/or Father Monitored Their School Work, by Racial/Ethnic Group

Racial/ethnic group	Mother	Father
Asian-Pacific	85	80
White	87	73
Black	87	52
Hispanic	87	66
American Indian	83	62

Acknowledgments

We gratefully acknowledge the following instructors, who kindly submitted some of their students' best work for this collection.

Gary Albrightson, University of North Dakota

Dawn Anderson, Wright State University

Steven Axelrod, University of California at Riverside

Amy Barber, Bowling Green State University

Jane Blakelock, Wright State University

David Bringhurst, Wright State University

Elizabeth Brisby, Wright State University

Angela Buehring, Southern Illinois University, Carbondale

Marilyn Carder, Wright State University

Christine Cetrulo, University of Kentucky

Robert Connors, University of New Hampshire

Wilfred O. Dietrich, Blinn College

Marvin Diogenes, University of Arizona

Thomas Domek, University of North Dakota

Edward A. Dougherty, Bowling Green State University

Kathleen Gould, University of North Carolina, Wilmington

Joan Hawthorne, University of North Dakota

Antoinette Hibbard, University of Oklahoma

Phyllis Hodson-Hutsell, Purdue University

Sandra Holmgren, University of North Dakota

Chrisa Hotchkiss, Bowling Green State University

Yi Arthur Jin, Bowling Green State University

Mary Kenton, Wright State University

Susan Koprince, University of North Dakota

Lisa Lewis-Spicer, University of North Dakota

Debbie Lindblom, Wright State University

Susan MacDonald, University of California at San Diego

Gary C. Minor, Seminole Community College

Dianna M. Myers, Wright State University

Thomas Palakeel, University of North Dakota

George Pollock, Blinn College

Kevin Price, University of North Dakota

Alan Rice, Bowling Green State University

Larry Rich, Wright State University

Lucy Schultz, University of Cincinnati

Jeri Thornton, University of Oklahoma

Mary Walker, University of North Dakota

Jean Waltman, Eastern Michigan University

Anne Whitaker, Wright State University

James H. Wilson, Trinidad State Junior College

Tammy Zambo, University of North Dakota

Richard Zbaracki, Iowa State University

A Note on the Copy-Editing

We all know that the work of professional writers rarely appears in print without first being edited. But what about student writing—especially essays that are presented *as models* of student writing? Do these get edited too?

This is not as clear-cut an issue as it may first appear. While it's easy to draw an analogy with professional writing and simply declare that "all published writing gets edited," there are some important differences between student and professional writing. For one thing, the student writing is presented *as student writing*. That is, it's offered to the reader as an example of the kind of writing students can and do produce in a writing class. And since most students don't have the benefit of a professional editor to read their work before it's graded, their work may not be as polished as the models they see in the text.

For another, students whose work appears in publications like these rarely have the opportunity to participate in the editorial process. Publication schedules being what they are, text authors and editors often don't know exactly what they want in terms of example essays until late in the process, and by then they may be so immersed in their own revising that it's difficult, if not impossible, to supervise 25 or more student writers as well.

For these reasons, student writers are usually simply asked to sign a statement, transferring to the publisher "all rights to my essay, subject to final editing by the publisher," and don't see their work again until it appears in print. That makes the situation somewhat problematic.

But publishing student essays without editing is equally problematic. Every composition teacher knows that even the best papers, the A+ essays, aren't perfect. But readers of published prose, accustomed to the conventions of Edited American

A Note on the Copy-Editing

English, aren't always so generous.* The shift in tense that may be seen as a simple lapse in a student narrative becomes a major distraction in a published piece. Rather than preserve that tense shift in the interest of "absolute fidelity" to the student's work, it is more in keeping with the spirit and purpose of the enterprise to edit the passage. After all, the rest of the evidence indicates that the student is a strong writer, and would likely accede to the change if it were called to his or her attention.

In this respect, editing student essays should be seen not as a violation of the student's work but as a courtesy to the writer. True, some essays require more editing than others — perhaps because the student did not have as much opportunity to revise — but none in this collection have been altered significantly. In fact, every attempt has been made to respect the student's choices.

To give you an inside look at the editing process, we reproduce here the originally submitted version of Erick Young's essay "Only She" (p. x), along with the St. Martin's editor's "blue pencil" markings. It might be interesting to compare this early version with the final edited version printed on pages 30–34. What changes were made, and why? Were all of them necessary? If you were the writer, how would you react to these changes?

Finally, if you are a writer whose work has undergone editorial revision — perhaps as a result of peer critique — you might think about how the process felt to you. Did you appreciate your editor's work? Resent it? What did you learn from it? If you're like most of us, you probably realized that it's natural to resist criticism, but necessary to accept it. In other words, you learned to think of yourself as a writer.

---

*At first glance, this may seem to contradict what the experts say. Joseph Williams, for instance, argues (and at the same time beautifully demonstrates) that readers are much more likely to detect "error" in student papers than in the work of published professionals (*Phenomenology of Style*). This is true for marginal errors, the ones that don't make a strong impression on the reader's consciousness, but as Williams himself concedes, some errors obtrude on our consciousness more than others — not necessarily because they are "worse" but because they are more noticeable — and it is the very fact that they often *aren't* serious problems that allows us to overlook them in student prose.

Sample Copy-Editing

Erick Young
Person Essay
Rewrite

Only She

Those <u>eyes</u>. Brown. No no, deep, dark brown. Hardly a
wrinkle around them. Soft, smooth ~~looking~~ skin. And those
eyebrows. Neither thick nor thin, just bold--two curve~~d~~s
punctuati~~on marks gracing~~ ring her facial expressions with a
certain something⊙ ~~extra accent~~. Surprise, amusement--up would shoot
one of the brows, the right one I believe, just slightly,
accompanied by a mischievous little smirk⊙ ~~that would curl
onto her lips.~~ Anger, irritation--up and inward shot both
brows, tightly pressed, followed by a sharp "Whaat d'ya
want?! Don't bother me!" She never really meant it though;
~~she~~ it was just her way of saying "hello." Even though she wore glasses
she could still see all, with or without them. Her deep,
dark brown eyes were no ordinary eyes; ~~little masses of flesh
and tissue,~~ no, within those deep wells rested a pair of
magic orbs, two miniature crystal balls that could peer
into your mind and read all your little thoughts. Some
thought she had psychic powers. She knew what you were
thinking, or at least ~~so many times,~~ always seemed to know she ~~knew~~ what I was
thinking, even ~~all of~~ my most complex, inexplicable thoughts. And
that was all that seemed to matter at the time. Only she,
only Sonia Koujakian, only Mrs. K.

I do not recall the first time I noticed her at
school, but Mrs. K was not one to blend into ~~the~~ a crowd⊙ ~~for
very long.~~ ⟨briskly⟩ ⟨walking⟩ across our school's rotunda. I
would see her, tall and lean, wearing a skirt and a mauve-

159

colored raincoat, holding a **stuffed** beige handbag in one

hand, and a bright red coffee pot in the other. She seemed

so confident, always looking straight ahead ~~rather than~~

~~down~~ as she walked about ~~the~~ school. Perhaps it was her

hair that first caught my eye. It was short, [a mix of] ~~almost~~

~~spiked, with its~~ light brown and gray~~, hairs~~ combed

slightly up [+ almost spiked⊙] Not the typical sort of hairstyle for an

English teacher at our school. It set her apart ~~though~~ and

made her look [,]dynamic. Already I knew that she was

somebody special.

The [PSAT] ~~beckon to take the Preliminary Scholastic Aptitude~~

~~Test~~ brought [her into my life] ~~us together briefly~~ for the first time[,]in my

sophomore year[⊙] ~~allowing me to get a small taste of Mrs.~~

~~K's personality.~~ Even though she was the senior English

teacher, she ~~made an open~~ offer[ed] to coach any undaunted

sophomores or juniors after school for the nefarious "<u>SAT</u>

jr." Trying to be the savvy student, I joined~~, two other~~

~~friends and accepted her offer. Only~~ a small group [who] ~~of us~~

gathered in her cove after[#]school ~~the following afternoons~~

~~and~~ [to]practiced[,] vocabulary drills and sentence completions.

Mrs. K would scold us on the finer points of grammar~~, when~~

[as]we reviewed our errors[⊙] ~~throwing at~~ [giving] us her "Come on, get

with the production!" ~~expression~~ [look] Not the typical reaction

from a [teacher;] ~~person one hardly knew; all the little formalities~~

~~I had come to expect in a teacher-student relationships~~

~~had been thrown out the window with Mrs. K;~~ She treated us

like peers, and would say to us what[ever] was on her mind

without ~~any~~ pretense[s] ~~, niceties,~~ [pleasantrys] or euphe[m]isms[,]. We could

do the same, if we had the [guts] ~~stomach~~ to try. Her casual

disposition made me feel both relaxed and nervous; ~~I did~~

160

Sample Copy-Editing

none of us knew

~~not know~~ how to act around her, whether to joke and tease

her, or respect and honor her. ~~Most of my friends felt the~~

~~same way.~~ We all ~~felt~~ agreed$ however, that she ~~simply~~ was ~~down-to-~~

~~Earth,~~ as down-to-Earth as they come, ~~friends, teachers,~~

~~or anyone. Soon, the prop sessions were over and it would~~

~~not be until~~ two years later, as an older and wiser senior,

~~that~~ I would get ~~the~~ a full ~~taste~~ dose of Mrs. K's personality.

My first day in Mrs. K's class left much to be

desired. I entered to find ~~Most of~~ my classmates just ~~sat around waiting,~~

~~talking,~~ laughing, and joking. The first-day-of-school jitters

had become passe', and ~~a certain~~ the smugness ~~automatically~~ that comes with

~~arising from the passage of four years and the arrival of~~

~~seniordom~~ dominated the room. It ~~I~~ was ~~amongst~~ a convention

of Alfred E. Neumans, and the nonchalant air of "What Me

Worry?" ~~wafted in~~ filled the classroom. Some ~~of my classmates,~~ students$

however, sat very quietly. ~~Some~~ These were ~~very~~ the wise ~~some had~~ ones; they'd

heard about Mrs. K~~before~~. Academic ~~hardships~~ tensions hovered like

the ~~an~~ inevitable black storm cloud above Room 5C3. There was

a small fear of the unknown and the unexpected nudging

about in my stomach as I sat at the far end of the center

table. Strange how this was the only classroom in the

entire building to have six huge wooden tables instead of

forty individual little desks; someone must have wanted it

that way. For once I was not too anxious to ~~be too close~~ sit up

~~to the~~ front. Suddenly ~~Soon~~ the chattery ~~atmosphere~~ ring diminished ~~into~~

~~nothingness.~~ Mrs. K was coming.

In she ambled, with her stuffed ~~beige~~ handbag and

bright red coffee pot, wearing a skirt and ~~her~~ the mauve

raincoat; she ~~it~~ was just as I had ~~imagined~~ remembered. She scanned the

room, and up went her right eyebrow. A most peculiar

161

"I-know-what-you-are-up-to" smirk was our first greeting. Now I was nervous.

"All right ladies and gentlemen, I want to see if you belong in my class," she began~~, in a soft but earnest voice.~~ "Take out a pen and lots of paper." Pause. "Now don't get too worried over this, since you are all geniuses anyway. You know, if you've got it you've got it, if you don't..." ~~Her shoulders~~ she shrugged. Pause. "Some of you know you don't really belong in here," she chided~~, as she~~ point~~ed~~ing her finger, "and it's time you stopped getting put in Honors English just because ~~you have a little star by your name in the role book, meaning~~ you passed some silly little test ~~way~~ back in second grade. Well now we're going to see what you can do." ~~she said matter-of-factly, arms akimbo, right brow up.~~ "Okay now, stop and think for a moment, and get those ~~wonderful~~ creative juices going. I want you to write me a paper telling me the origin of the English language. You can be as creative as you want. Make up something if you have to, two cavemen grunting at each other, I don't care. You have until the end of the period. Go."

It was not the most encouraging welcome. For a moment the who class just sort of slumped in their seats, suddenly drained ~~phased and drained~~ of all vitality and hopes of a relaxed senior year. Blank faces abounded, Mine included, ~~was one of them.~~ I had no idea what to write. The origin of the English language? Being "creative" seemed too risky. What ever happened to the good 'ol five paragraph essay with specific examples? Well I didn't have any specific examples anyway. I remember staring at a sheet of white paper, then scrawling down some incoherent mumbo-jumbo. I

wanted to impress her, too much. ~~I choked, and was doomed to a dismal dungeon of drudgery. I blew it with Mrs. K.~~

"It was nice knowing you," I signed as I handed in my

paper. What a first day.

That first day ~~of class~~ with Mrs. K would not be my last ~~with Mrs. K~~ fortunately. ~~A poor performance on the first pressure writing was not a notice of termination but rather an early warning of possible eviction.~~ Although the class size shrunk

the following days as some students ran for their academic

lives, I, was not prepared to leave. I knew Mrs. K's class

would be an arduous English journey, but I could never let

myself miss it. It would be a journey well worth taking.

As the weeks continued, tidbits of Mrs. K's colorful

past and philosophy about life would somehow always creep

into ~~our~~ lectures and class discussions. We found out she

had served as a volunteer nurse in a combat hospital in Japan ~~based combat hospital~~ and had "seen it all," even grown men cry." During

the '60s a wider Mrs. K could be seen cruising the streets

of San Francisco on ~~atop~~ motorcycle, decked out in long

spiked boots and short spiked hair. She later traded in

her motorcycle and boots for a Fiat and white Reeboks. ~~though.~~ And there was a running joke about her age. Mrs. K

could not be much less ~~younger~~ than ~~her mid-forties~~ 45, but just

as Jack Benny was forever 49, she was forever 28. One of

her T-shirts said so. Twenty-eight was a good year, ~~for her~~ she

would tell us, but never quite explained why.

I would come to deeply trust and respect this

~~seemingly~~ eccentric lady. ~~while the school year progressed.~~

I guess I have Oedipus Rex to thank for our first close

meeting. We had to compose an extensive essay on the Oedipus Trilogy, (much of ~~which~~) on which our semester grade would be based. Foolishly, I chose to write on the most ~~difficult~~ abstract topic, ~~concerning~~ predestination and divine justice. I toiled for days, ~~inflicting upon~~ torturing myself ~~a sort deranged mental torture~~ trying to come ~~to~~ up with some definitive conclusions. Finally, I realized by struggle was merely carrying my mind farther and farther adrift in a sea of confusion. I needed someone to rescue me; I needed Mrs. K.

We arranged to meet in the Faculty Commons, a small smoky room of teachers with ~~their~~ red pens at work and administrators shooting the breeze over lunch. I crept inside with notes in hand and took a seat, ~~amongst the hasa.~~ She soon arrived, holding a tuna-on-wheat, a chocolate chip cookie, and the red coffee pot. "I hope you don't mind if I eat while we ~~discuss~~ talk," she ~~mentioned offhandly,~~ said, "but if you do, I'm going to eat anyway." Smile.

We talked the whole lunch period. I felt awkward at first, actually struggling to explain why ~~I was~~ I'd been struggling with the assignment ~~before.~~ But then Mrs. K the Mentor emerged--soft spoken, introspective, wise. I opened up to her. We sat beside ~~one another~~ each other at that table, reflecting on predestination, divine justice, and life. A ray of sunshine cut through ~~my~~ clouds of confusion. Our reflections were interrupted by the lunch bell, but ~~later~~ continued after school. Two days and two drafts later, I had gained more than just a deep understanding of Oedipus Rex; I had gained a friend. What was it about this woman that enabled me to reveal a different part of myself? Never before had I ~~ever~~ spoken so openly about my thoughts, ~~and~~ or about myself. Most people did not understand ~~what I was contemplating.~~ *my cares and thoughts⊙* But she

understood. ~~Oftentimes I did not have to explain much, her crystal balls would perform their magic.~~

    I would go back to room 5C3 many afternoons later to sort my thoughts. To her I was no longer Erick but Hamlet, ~~deemed~~ *because of* my pensive and complex nature. "Okay Hamlet, what's on your mind?" our conversations would begin. ~~It seemed~~ every writing assignment became an excuse to spend time after*#*school talking and reflecting, ~~with just~~ me at the wood table, ~~and she~~ *her* at her stool. We digressed on everything from Paradise Lost to Shakespeare to ~~Robert Frost's~~ "The Road Not Taken" ~~these many afternoons.~~ Sometimes other students would come ~~afterschool~~ for help on their papers, ~~but~~ *and* I would always let them go first, so that I could be the last left. ~~Sometimes~~ *Often* I would ~~receive small lessons in life afterschool.~~ *learn about more* "Life's not black and white, it's a hazy gray, and you've always got to use that wonderful piece of machinery God gave you and question things because nothing is clear cut~~, and learn more about this world~~ (than just literature.) I noticed my perceptions changing, as well as my writing style. More of my character entered my writing, and the Mr. Detached Impartiality persona I once favored faded into the background. Being "creative" no longer seemed risky. She told me to put more of myself in my creations, and I listened.

    near ~~Towards~~ the ~~close~~ *end* of my senior year, I asked her about her favorite novel, ~~during~~ (one ~~last~~ afternoon) "Oh, without a doubt, Les Miserables," she replied. "But I never could find an unedited version." ~~Three days later at the end of~~

On
⟨in⟩   ⟨ing⟩
⌃Graduation Day, ~~while~~ a sea of ~~teary-eyed~~ seniors hugged
⟨mortarboards sailing⟩
one another⌃ and red and blue ~~motorboards~~ ~~sailed~~ through
the air⌃ ~~I searched through the crowd for Mrs. K, and~~
handed her a small box. ~~Wrapped~~ inside with a ~~card, and a~~
⟨of⟩
long thank-you on the cover⌃ was a new copy⌃ Les
Miserables, unedited and unabridged.

⟨that⟩
    I doubt⌃ I will come across many others like Mrs. K ~~in~~
~~my life.~~ Only she would sit with me one-on-one, and review
every minute detail of a draft. Only she would give up
~~many~~ an afternoon (to just) ~~sit down~~ shoot the breeze. Only
she could I call a mentor, a confidant, and a friend. I
still think of Mrs. K. Sometimes, when the pressures of
college come crashing down, and the order of life seems to
have run amok, I go to my room and slowly close the door
and my eyes, sit down, and talk with Mrs. K.

    "Okay Hamlet, what's on your mind..."

Submitting Papers for Publication

To Students and Instructors

We hope that this collection of essays is the first of many editions, and that we'll be able to include more essays from more colleges and universities in the next edition. Please let us see essays written using *The St. Martin's Guide* you'd like us to consider. Send them with this Paper Submission Form and the Agreement Form on the back to Marilyn Moller, St. Martin's Press, 175 Fifth Avenue, New York, NY 10010.

Paper Submission Form

Instructor's Name _____

School _____

Address _____

Department _____

Student's Name _____

Course _____

Writing activity the paper represents _____

This writing activity appears in chapter(s) _____
of *The St. Martin's Guide to Writing*

167

Agreement Form

I hereby transfer to St. Martin's Press all rights to my essay,

_____

(tentative title), subject to final editing by the publisher. These rights include copyright and all other rights of publication and reproduction. I guarantee that this essay is wholly my original work, and that I have not granted rights in it to anyone else.

FOR ST. MARTIN'S PRESS:

_____   X _____

Please type:

_____
Name

_____
Address

_____

_____
Phone

Please indicate the reader or publication source you assumed for your essay: _____

Write a few sentences about the purpose or purposes of your essay. What did you hope to achieve with your reader?

_____

_____

_____

_____